*The Golden Age
of Spiritual Writing*

Lancelot Andrewes

The Private Prayers

Selected and translated by
David Scott

SPCK

Published in Great Britain in 2002
Society for Promoting Christian Knowledge
Holy Trinity Church
Marylebone Road
London NW1 4DU

British Library Cataloguing-in-Publication Data
A catalogue record for this book is available from the British Library

ISBN 0-281-05440-1

10 9 8 7 6 5 4 3 2 1

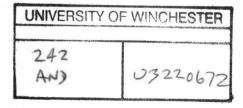
Typeset by FiSH Books, London
Printed in Great Britain by Antony Rowe Ltd, Chippenham, Wiltshire

In memory of
Bishop Donald Coggan
(Archbishop of Canterbury 1974–1980)
who shared a devotion with
Lancelot Andrewes
for preaching and praying
the Word

and to Jean, his wife,
my loving thanks.

Contents

The Golden Age of Spiritual Writing

The Golden Age of Spiritual Writing brings together a series of books of English 'spiritual' poetry and prose, selected and introduced by well-known contemporary authors and scholars. Many of the writers on whom this series focuses flourished during the seventeenth century. You may well ask, 'Why concentrate on writers of the seventeenth century? Wasn't it a long time ago?' Historically, that period might well seem 'a long time ago', especially when we consider the huge changes in communications and in scientific understanding, and, yet, looked at with the long view of human history, the seventeenth century is quite recent. It was, in many ways, the beginning of the modern age. We share with the people of that time the struggles and strains of being human, the joys as well as the challenges of the natural world, and the seemingly incontrovertible facts of birth and death. In our religious lives, too, we want to talk about the challenges of new cultures bearing down on what we consider eternal truths, and the relationship between different Christian traditions.

But we do bother about the seventeenth-century writers, and have done with increasing enthusiasm since the early part of the twentieth century, with the name and influence of T. S. Eliot ranking large. I think we bother about them for three main reasons. First, they write well. Second, they tell eternal truths. And third, for our spiritually bewildered age, they fill a dry well with clear, fresh water.

There is something about the English language of this period that has an element of the miraculous. We find this most commonly in the plays of Shakespeare and in the Authorized Version of the Bible: the two books without which any stay on a desert island is deficient. Their language is not so removed from our own that we are utterly confused by it, but it is freshly coined enough to retain its life, its bite and chew. It has the power to evoke in us, physically, the moods, emotions and thoughts the words are trying to express. The words and the rhythms can make us cry and laugh and ponder with a huge intensity. Someone could probably explain this miracle and find it, for sure, in other writers of different ages; but all I want to do is to encourage readers to see if it is true for them about the seventeenth century. However, when it comes to dealing with the translated material of Lancelot Andrewes then different linguistic criteria have to be applied.

The words have to be about something. It is not just a matter of style or sound. The words have to tell us something that we find valuable. This series concentrates on spiritual writers. Each of them refers easily and unashamedly to God, and not infrequently to Jesus Christ as the revelation of God's love in and for the world. They write of sin and prayer, of salvation and love, of death and heaven and hell, and they mean real things by them. The writers precede the growth of rationalism that developed in the eighteenth century. Are we not too grown up and too clever for such things? Are we not, as Eliot put it, banging an antique drum? Each of the books in this series will be at pains to persuade us that this is not so, and more importantly, the writers themselves will do so, too. They take the great spiritual themes of all times and places: desire, fear, decision-making, a sense of wonder and of awe, anxiety and loss, and, by their own vision and breadth of experience, make them reach down to us in our own day.

Reading the great classics of spiritual literature of whatever age today will always be a new thing, it is a new generation that is reading them. Reading Traherne in an era of massive pollution will put his sense of wonder and affection for the natural world in a new political context. Donne's honesty about sex and religion will raise questions about the nature of humanity, which, after Freud, will seem as real as ever. Herbert's gentle, pragmatic ethics might encourage a new generation to reflect on standards of behaviour and the place of an ordered life in a free-floating world. Each of the writers presented in this series will have something to contribute to the contemporary debate. Pondering these questions will be to the benefit of both writer and reader. The echoes of great literature come not only from within the text itself, but also from outside the text. In reading the poetry, the thoughts, the prayers, we make them live again. For people searching for the words that express what they want to say, here in this series will be some familiar resources and, I trust, some revelations.

As editor of the series, I would like to thank all the authors who agreed to contribute. I am especially grateful for the high quality of their work, which has made my task so much easier. I have worked closely throughout with the editorial team at SPCK, especially with Liz Marsh. I am immensely grateful to them for their friendly support and for their decision to take on the publication of this fascinating area of spiritual writing. Without them this series would never have come together.

David Scott
Winchester

Introduction

Beginnings

I first came across the prayers of Lancelot Andrewes in a small book I now know to have been one in a series of Methuen classics. It must have been a cheap book back in the 1950s for an ardent schoolboy to have bought out of limited pocket money. I think I gave it away when I had collected other editions, so that somebody else could discover the riches of the *Preces Privatae*, as it is most generally called. From that palm-sized edition I took a sentence or two to heart. Here is one on the Holy Spirit:

> the calling out of the
> the hallowing in of the } Universal
>
> (Tuesday: Faith, p. 56)

Notice the outrageous lack of finish, the fleeting quality of it, the body language which was also the language of the spirit, and those wonderful brackets which I so enjoyed copying with their swirls. The second memorable line was:

> The old man is covered up in a thousand wrappings
> (from An Evening Reflection, p. 97)

I don't know who, or why, or where it went from there, but I knew that person was me, that was my state. Andrewes had found me.

The influence of T. S. Eliot

For many years those few words were enough. That is, until I came across Andrewes again, in the poetry and essays of T. S. Eliot. Eliot's work among the writers of the sixteenth and seventeenth centuries led him to be much influenced by the style and subject matter of this most Anglican of Divines, Bishop Lancelot Andrewes (1555–1626). It was from the sermons that Eliot took quotations, more than from the prayers. For example, his use of Andrewes's Nativity Sermon for Christmas 1619, on the text of the visit of the Magi to Jesus, became the inspiration for Eliot's poem, *The Journey of the Magi*. Feeling that I wasn't a completely lone wolf in valuing the work of Andrewes, Eliot kept me to the hunt, and searching for a more comprehensive version of the prayers brought me to the great 1903 edition which was F. E. Brightman's editorial work, *The Private Devotions of Lancelot Andrewes*. It was 'great', because at that time it was easily the most comprehensive edition, with a very good introduction, notes and biblical references for almost every word in the text, which helped in tracing the line of Andrewes's thought.

Lancelot Andrewes the man

Lancelot Andrewes was born in London in 1555, the eldest of twelve children. His father was a mariner. He was sent to school in the city at The Merchant Taylors' School where, under Richard Mulcaster's headship, he learnt the languages of the scriptures: Greek, Latin, and Hebrew. He was a tall, long-headed, serious boy, but school work was not his only love, because he also enjoyed walking. When he went to Pembroke College, Cambridge to continue his studies, he liked to do the journey from London to Cambridge on foot. His connections with his College were very important for him, and he stayed on there as a teacher, later becoming Fellow of the College, and Catechist. From Cambridge he went back to London to be Vicar of St Giles Cripplegate, and also a Canon of St Paul's where he continued his teaching ministry through lecture and sermon. His sermons became famous and most influential.

It is through his involvement in the translation of the Authorized Version of the Bible that he is best remembered. The translation work was done by a series of committees set up by King James I, and Andrewes, then Dean of Westminster, was the convenor of the group to which was assigned the translation of Genesis to 2 Kings. From his early days at school, Andrewes had shown a facility for languages and had mastered completely the three great biblical languages of Hebrew, Latin and Greek. When he prayed, he prayed in the original biblical languages.

The Privateness of the prayers

His private prayers first saw the light of day in Greek and Hebrew, then in Latin, and only later in English. But we must tread carefully now: 'Private Prayers'? Who knows how people pray privately, if it really is private? Are these prayers of Andrewes really so private? The title *Private Prayers* (Latin, *Preces Privatae*) was attached to these writings in the first English translation of 1647: *Private Devotions by the Right Reverend Father in God Lancelot Andrewes, late Bishop of Winchester*. Andrewes had died in 1626, twenty years earlier. We have to do quite a lot more detective work to uncover the genesis of these writings. One thing is certain: Andrewes did not live to see the general dissemination of the material that went under his name as private prayers. It is likely, however, that he was responsible for the first manuscript copying of a selection of these prayers.

We must imagine a man, a bishop, whose life was intensely given over to study, prayer and preaching. Those who knew him well, and these included the King James I, encouraged the dissemination of his sermons and lectures. The public writings became well known, and so there came to be an interest in how Bishop Andrewes, who all his life encouraged others to pray, prayed himself.

The Laud Manuscript

Towards the end of his life, when he was Bishop of Winchester, Andrewes wrote down a scheme of prayer that included prayers for each day of the week, with some supplementary material for early morning and late evening. He wrote it in Greek, in a notebook, five by two-and-a-half inches – about the size of his own hand – and bound in white vellum. Andrewes gave this book to William Laud, who was then Bishop of Bath and Wells, but later became Archbishop of Canterbury, and was beheaded in 1645. On the cover of the book William Laud wrote, 'My reverend Friend Bishop Andrewes gave me this Booke a little before his death. W: Bathe et Welles'. It now resides, in a box inside a box, in the Bodleian Library, Oxford: a beautiful object to hold and turn the pages of, and numinous to read. This manuscript is known as the Laud Manuscript, and it is the manuscript from which I have taken and translated the prayers in the first section of this book.

For the prayers for the days of the week I have tried to reproduce as closely as possible the layout of the Laud Manuscript. This is to give the reader some idea of the immediacy of the original, and of how the prayers were designed to be seen on the page. We can see how Andrewes's own mind was working as he wrote them, with their lists, the inclusion of parts of Orthodox liturgies, and the use of medieval Latin prayers, much as we might make up a commonplace book ourselves. I have added the headings – commemoration, penitence, acts of grace, profession of faith, hope, intercessions, blessings – in order to give the book some sort of order, as editors have done since the seventeenth century.

When John Henry Newman left Oxford in 1842 and went to live at Littlemore, a village outside Oxford, he translated the Greek prayers of Andrewes. His translations run like the waters of the Cherwell under Magdalen Bridge, smooth and mellifluous. His *Greek Devotions of Bishop Andrews, Translated and Arranged* is like a well-rounded, epic poem. It was printed for Rivingtons in 1843 and sold for 2d a sheet. I have followed Newman's softer and smoother precedent for the early morning and late night prayers on the understanding that at such times one needs all the help one can get to read with as little effort as possible.

The Lambeth Palace Manuscript
That accounts for the main part of this particular selection of prayers. Always with collections of Andrewes's prayers, though,

there is a considerable amount of other material, usually written in Latin. The Laud Manuscript was a handwritten manuscript in Greek, probably from the 1620s. It now gets more complicated. In 1670 an edition of the prayers was printed in book form, and this included both the Greek material that was known from manuscripts, and also Latin material gathered from earlier manuscripts. In a sense, most of the known material then available was included in this edition, and could well have been entitled 'The Collected Prayers of...'. It was actually called *Rev. Patris Lanc. Andrews Episc. Winton. Preces Privatae Graece & Latine.*

Why did Andrewes write his prayers in both Greek and Latin? I think that the primitive, earliest manuscript of the prayers, the Laud Manuscript, was a very special production and conveys Andrewes's deep love of New Testament Greek, the language in which the words of Christ first came to his Church. He probably prayed most deeply in Greek. Yet there was also much material in Latin circulating because that was the theological and learned language of the seventeenth century. A lot of Andrewes's writings were in Greek, and many of his scattered uncollected jottings, notes, sermon plans and lecture frameworks were in Latin. But the early Latin manuscripts have never been discovered, except in very small selections. Even when Brightman made his magisterial edition in 1903, there was no major Latin manuscript to hand.

It is only in the last few years that a significant Latin manuscript has come to light. This manuscript, again in what we would call book form, was bought by the Lambeth Palace Library in 1994. The material that this manuscript contains is not unknown from other printed sources – a great deal of it appears in the 1670 printed book mentioned above – but to see the handwritten, manuscript version of the prayer is most interesting. It gives evidence of the prayers in use as early as the 1640s.

The manuscript is believed to be in the handwriting of Gilbert Sheldon, Archbishop of Canterbury, 1663–77. Sheldon was a friend of William Laud's who spent most of the Commonwealth period (1640s) in the Midlands. The manuscript with the Latin prayers in it, and also some English material, was known to have been in use by Sheldon at the family home of the Shirleys, at Staunton Harold in Leicestershire. We know this because in addition to the Andrewes prayers, there are prayers in another hand, particularly to do with the confirmation of the young Shirley boys. The second section of prayers in this book are from this Lambeth Palace manuscript. They include a Meditation on the Passion, prayers inspired by the Lord's prayer, some occasional prayers, and the penitential prayers based on the Ten Commandments – some of the few prayers written in English. Notice the seventeenth-century spelling.

Andrewes, a man of prayer

I suppose, with books of prayers, we could well say about the way we read them, 'Let's leave that up to the Holy Spirit'. The Holy Spirit will direct people to the prayers; such was my early experience of Andrewes's prayers. Even so, here are some thoughts on the use of these prayers in our daily lives. When Andrewes was alive, conditions of life were rather different. I feel sure there would have been less general background noise, less 'white noise', always there but coming from an invisible source. There would have been fewer distractions, and a slower pace of life that enabled Andrewes to spend long hours in prayer. Musicians practising concert pieces are familiar with long hours of practice – four, five, six hours a day is not unusual for them. Similarly with Andrewes: it is recorded that he spent four or five hours a day in private prayer. Life is not like that for most of us, and there is a danger that we try and 'do' all of Andrewes's prayers at one sitting, reading the book through as if it were a novel. If we attempt that we will easily get clogged. A short phrase that sticks, or just one of the prayers from the daily collections, is often enough for us in a time of prayer.

Andrewes was a methodical man. He would have used the daily Morning and Evening Prayer from the Book of Common Prayer of his day. He would have said these in his episcopal chapel, his secretaries and friends joining him. In addition, he is likely to have said, when his duties allowed him, the daily hours of prayer, to make up the biblical 'seven times a day do I praise you' (Ps. 119). To these additional times of prayer he would have added material from the medieval and orthodox traditions, and from the early collections of the church compiled from the fourth century onwards. His methodical nature is mirrored in the order of the daily private prayers. They begin with a quotation from scripture suitable to the early morning, which suggests that they were used on rising from bed. This is quickly followed by a brief meditation or commemoration of the creative activity of God as described in the first chapter of Genesis. So Sunday (the first day) commemorates the giving of the light, and Saturday (the seventh day) commemorates the rest of God at the completion of his work. The first day is always Sunday for Andrewes. In the ascription of his prayers he always used numbers, and even sometimes symbols for the day, not the conventional, perhaps rather secular, names. Then there is a time of confession, helped by the words of some of the famous biblical confessions, of Ezekiel, and Jeremiah, the Samaritan woman, and the Debtor. This is followed by a short prayer for grace to live a good life. Then comes a personalized profession of faith, the creed prayed through rather than just proclaimed. Intercession, or praying for others, which comes next, played a very important part in Andrewes's life of prayer (is there anything he doesn't remember to pray for?), and this concludes with a time of blessing, commendation and praise.

Around these prayers we must imagine the silence and reflection of a life devoted to an interior dialogue with God. All we have here are the words on the page, interestingly shaped to reflect the progression of thought and prayer, but words just the same. Therefore we have to use our imaginations to put in the meditative silence which would surely for Andrewes have accompanied the words. From his private journals and papers come some cries of deepest remorse. He reflects on the aridity of his soul, and calls it, with the psalmist, a dried-up shard of broken pottery, and yet he can also soar to the heights of praise with the words of the Te Deum, 'Holy, holy, holy, Lord God of Hosts.

Heaven and earth are full of the majesty of your glory. Blessed be the glory of the Lord, rising from his place.'

You will notice that the tone of the prayers is consistently biblical. In his edition Brightman put in every possible biblical, liturgical and secular reference, and that has been very useful for my work, but is not necessary for this book. At the start it is enough to be caught by a word or a phrase. The cross-references, and the variety of translations, is for later, if at all. Andrewes gets a word or theme in his head, like 'hope', and his mind then scours the Bible, like a wordsearch on a computer, and that word is filled out with all the characters of the scriptures who leant on that word, and their situations. Another dimension would have been added as he reflected on the translations of the word in different languages. So the word, as it did in his sermons, becomes a crystal, turning in the light for the light to scintillate. He turns a word until the light transforms it into 'the Word', the person in whose life and nature all language rests its case, and receives its meaning, even Jesus Christ. In one of his sermons Andrewes called the infant Jesus, 'the Word who could not speak a word'.

Ten years ago, when I came to Winchester, I decided to try and make an accessible translation of the prayers. I remember, in my youthful enthusiasm, organizing midday prayers just so that I could pray the prayers of Andrewes with others. On the first day my wife and one faithful elderly lady joined me, and we went through the prayers for that day. This excellent beginning did not maintain its momentum in any public sense. Yet, slowly and surely, with such excitements on the way as the printing of a small part of the Daily Prayers on Chip Coakley's Jericho Press in 1993, and Bishop Donald Coggan presenting me with his own copy of the 1692 edition of the prayers, we have come to this point. It may not be the end of the journey, but it is for me a milestone, and I am extremely happy to share the fruits of a labour of love with you.

I am very grateful to the staffs of the Bodleian Library and the Lambeth Palace Library for making the texts available for translation.

The Dial

You who hold all times and seasons in your hand:
  grant that we may make our prayers to you
    at such a convenient time that you may be found,

                and save us.

You, Lord, who for us and for our salvation
  was born at the dead of night:
  give us daily to be born again of the Holy Spirit
    until Christ is formed in us most perfectly,

                and save us.

Very early in the morning you rose from the dead:
  raise us daily to newness of life,
    prompting us to those ways of repentance
    that you best can teach us,

                and save us.

At nine o'clock in the morning, the third hour,
  you sent your Holy Spirit upon your Apostles:
    take not the Holy Spirit from us,
    but daily renew the same within us,

                and save us.

At midday, at the sixth hour, and on the sixth day,
  you nailed the sins of the world,
    with yourself to the cross:
    blot out the handwriting of our sins
      which writes our condemnation, and set it aside,

                and save us.

At midday, you let down a great sheet from Heaven to earth,
  an image of your Church:
    receive us up into it, sinners of the gentiles,
    and with it, receive us up together, into Heaven,

                                          and save us.

At one o'clock in the afternoon, you willed that the fever should
  leave the nobleman's son:
    if any thing of fever, or of sickness, in our souls
      should rest on us, take it away,

                                          and save us.

At three o'clock, the ninth hour, for us sinners,
  and for our sins you tasted death:
    destroy whatever in us draws us to the world,
      and whatever is contrary to your will,

                                          and save us.

You who willed that the ninth hour should be an hour of prayer:
  hear us while we pray in this hour,
    and help us to obtain our prayer and our desires,

                                          and save us.

At four o'clock, the tenth hour, you willed your apostle
  to rejoice with great joy, and caused him to say,
    'We have found the Messiah!'
  Help us in the same way to find the Messiah,
    and when we have found him, in like manner to rejoice,

                                          and save us.

At evening time you willed to be taken down from the cross
  and placed in the tomb:
    take our sins away from us, and bury them in the sepulchre,
      covering with good works whatever we have done amiss,

                                          and save us.

You who even at the eleventh hour of the day,
  sent workers into the vineyard and fixed their wage,
    even though they had stood idle all day in the market place:
      grant us a like favour, and though it be late,
        about the eleventh hour,
      accept us graciously when we return to you,
                        and save us.

You who at the hour of supper willed to institute
  the most sacred mysteries of your body and blood:
    keep our memories alive with those mysteries, and help us
      share in them, and in them never for judgement
        but for the forgiveness of sins,
      and to receive the benefits of the new covenant,
                        and save us.

Late at night, by your breath upon them,
  you conferred authority on your Apostles,
  to forgive and to retain sins: allow us
  to share in that authority,
  not for the keeping of our sins but for the forgiving of the same,
                        and save us.

You awakened both David the Prophet and Paul the Apostle
  to praise you at this midnight hour:
    give us also songs to praise you, to remember
      you upon our beds,
                        and save us.

At midnight you warned that the Bridegroom would come:
  grant that the call, 'The Bridegroom is coming!'
    may sound continually in our ears, that we may never
      be left unprepared,
                        and save us.

By the crowing of the cock you shamed your apostle
  into penitence: grant us at this same hour,
    the shame to go out and weep bitterly,
      for those things we have done to your shame,
                      and save us.

You told us you would come to be our judge,
  not when we were ready, but
    at the time we least expected:
      prepare us every day to be ready for your coming,
                      and save us.

The Laud Manuscript

On Prayer

Samuel among those who call upon your name.

Ps. 99.6

As for me, God forbid
    that I should sin against the Lord
    in ceasing to pray
    before God for you,
    and to teach you the way,
    good and right.

1 Sam. 12.23

But we will give ourselves continually to prayer,
    and to the ministry of the word.

Acts 6.4

To you that answer prayer shall vows be paid,
to you shall all flesh come to confess their sins.
    When my misdeeds prevail against me,
      you will purge them away.

Ps. 65.2, 3

    You will open my lips, O Lord:
and my mouth shall proclaim your praise.

Ps. 51.15

Times of Prayer

Always,
  without ceasing,
  at all times.

He knelt down three times a day and
prayed and gave thanks before his God,
as was his custom.

Dan. 6.10

In the evening and morning and midday I will pray
  and he will hear my voice.

Ps. 15.18

Seven times a day will I praise you:
1 in the morning, a long time before day
2 when I was waking
3 at the third hour of the day
4 about the sixth hour
5 at the hour of prayer, being the ninth hour
6 at evening
7 by night,
    at midnight.

Prayers at the Beginning of the Day

On Waking

You it is who sends the light and creates
the morning,
causing the sun to rise on the good
and on the evil:
lighten the blindness of our minds
with the knowledge of the truth.

Let your face so shine upon us,
that in your light we may see light,
and, at the last, may the light
of the grace that is, be transformed
into the light of the glory
that shall be.

Acclamation

Glory to you, O Lord, glory to you,
glory to you who have given me sleep
for the refreshing of my weakness,
and to restore the labours
of this fretful body.

To this day and all days,
a perfect, peaceful, healthy, sinless course:
let us ask of the Lord.

An angel of peace, a faithful guide,
  guardian of soul and body,
    to pitch a tent around me,
and always to prompt what brings salvation:
    let us ask of the Lord.

Pardon and remission
of all sins and offences:
    let us ask of the Lord.

To our souls, what is good and convenient,
  and peace to the world:
    let us ask of the Lord.

Repentance and discipline
  for the rest of our life,
and health and peace to the end:
    let us ask of the Lord.

Whatever is true, whatever is honest,
  whatever just, whatever pure,
whatever lovely, whatever of good report,
  if there be any virtue, any praise,
    such thoughts, such deeds:
    let us ask of the Lord.

A Christian close,
  without sin, without shame,
and if it please you without pain,
  and a good answer
at the awesome and testing judgement-seat
  of JESUS CHRIST our Lord:
    let us ask of the Lord.

Confession

Essence beyond essence, Nature uncreate,
    Framer of the world,
    I set you, Lord, before my face,
    and I lift up my soul to you.

    I worship you on my knees,
and humble myself under your mighty hand.

    I smite my breast
    and say with the Publican,
God be merciful to me a sinner,
    the chief of sinners;
    to a sinner worse than the Publican,
be merciful to me, as to the Publican.

    Father of mercies,
    I beseech your fatherly love,
    do not despise me,
the unclean worm, the dead dog, the putrid corpse,
    despise not the work of your own hands,
    nor your own image
    though marred by sin.

Lord, if you will, you can make me clean.
Lord, only say the word, and I shall be clean.

    And O my Saviour Christ,
    Christ my Saviour,
Saviour of sinners, of which I am chief,
    despise me not, Lord, despise me not,
    for I am called by your name.

    Look on me with those eyes
    with which you looked on

Mary Magdalen at the meal,
on Peter warming himself at the fire,
and at the thief on the cross,
that with the thief I may pray to you humbly
'Remember me, O Lord, when you come into your kingdom';

that with Peter I may weep bitterly and say,
'O that my eyes were a fountain of tears
that I might weep day and night';
that with Mary Magdalen I may hear you say,
'Your sins be forgiven you',
and that with her I may love much, because
my many sins have been forgiven.

And Lord,
all-holy, good, and life-giving Spirit,
despise not, O breath of life,
despise not your own holy things;
but turn again, Lord, at the last,
and be gracious to your servant.

Commendation

Blessed are you, Lord our God,
you turn the shadow of death into morning,
and renew the face of the earth.
You roll the darkness from the face of the light,
making the night to pass that brings on the day;
you have lightened my eyes,
that I sleep not in death;
delivering me from the terror by night,
from the pestilence that stalks in darkness;
you have driven sleep from my eyes,
and slumber from my eyelids;
you make the dawn and dusk to sing for joy:

I lay down and slept and rose up again,
and it was you Lord, only, that made me dwell in safety.
I woke, and look, my sleep was sweet to me.

Sweep away my transgressions like mist,
    and as a cloud my sins.
  Make me a child of the light, a child of the day,
to walk soberly, purely, honestly, as in the day.
  Vouchsafe to keep me this day without sin
    that I may be upheld when I fall,
    and lifted up when I am bowed down,
    that I may not harden my heart
    when I am tested and put to the proof,
    or made stubborn by the wiles of sin.

    Deliver me this day:
from the snare of the hunter, and the deadly pestilence,
  from the arrow that flies by day
    and the sickness that destroys in the noonday.

    Defend the day against my evil,
and against the evil of this day, defend me.

Let not my days be brought to an end like a breath
    nor my years in sudden terror.
One day pours out its song to another,
let this day unfold knowledge to the next.
  Let me hear of your loving kindness in the morning,
    for I put my trust in you.
  Show me the way that I should walk in,
for I lift up my soul to you.

    Save me, O Lord, from my enemies,
      for I run to you.
  Teach me to do the thing that pleases you,
    for you are my God;

let your loving Spirit lead me out
into the land of righteousness.

Give me life, O Lord, for your name's sake,
and for your righteousness' sake
bring my soul out of trouble;
remove foolish imaginations from me,
and inspire those which are good
and pleasing in your sight.

Turn away my eyes lest they look on vain things;
let my eyes look before me,
and my eyelids straight ahead.

Hedge round my ears with thorns
so they are deaf to harmful words.
Set my ear to hear right early,
and open my ears to hear the instruction of your words.

Set a watch, Lord, before my mouth,
to guard the door of my lips.
Let my words be seasoned with salt,
that they may minister grace to those who hear.

Let no deed become a grief to me,
nor an offence within my heart.
Let me do some work,
which will allow you to remember me, Lord, for good,
and spare me in the abundance of your mercy.

Into your hands, O Lord God of truth, I commend
my spirit, soul, and body.
You have created, redeemed and renewed them,
and with me, all mine, and all things mine.
You have given them to me, Lord,
in your goodness.

Guard us from all evil,
  guard our souls,
 I beseech you, O Lord.
Guard us so we do not fall,
and place us perfect
   in the presence of your glory
    on that day.

Preserve my going out and my coming in
  from this day forward and for evermore.
 Prosper, I pray, your servant this day,
   and grant me mercy
 in the sight of those who meet me.
  O God, make speed to save me,
  O Lord, make haste to help me.
   Turn to me,
    and have mercy on me.
  Give strength to your servant
 and help to the child of your handmaid.
  Show me some token of good,
that those who hate me may see it and be turned,
 because you, Lord, have helped me,
   and comforted me.

Prayers for the Days of the Week

The First Day:
Sunday

Through the tender compassion of our God
heaven's dawn has broken upon us.

Luke 1.78

Commemoration

A Glory to you, O Lord, glory to you,
who made the light, and enlightened the world.
You are the Lord who has given us light, even:

the visible light $\left\{ \begin{array}{l} \text{the beam of the sun} \\ \text{the flame of fire} \end{array} \right.$

$\left\{ \begin{array}{l} \text{by day and by night} \\ \text{in the evening and the morning} \end{array} \right.$

You are the Lord who has given us light, even:

the light of the mind
illuminating what can be known of God

in $\left\{ \begin{array}{l} \text{the writings of the law} \\ \text{the oracles of prophets} \\ \text{the melody of the psalms} \\ \text{the wisdom of proverbs} \\ \text{the experience of histories} \end{array} \right.$

You are the Lord who has given us light, even:

the light which never sets

B　　　　　　By your resurrection
　　　　　raise us to newness of life,
　　　setting us on the path to repentance.

May the God of peace
who brought back from the dead
the great Shepherd of the sheep,
by the blood of an everlasting covenant,
our Lord Jesus Christ,
make us perfect in every good work to do his will,
working in us that which is well pleasing in his sight
through Jesus Christ
to whom be glory for ever and ever.

C　　　　　O you who sent down this day
　　　　　your thrice holy Spirit
　　　　　on your disciples;
　　　take it not away from us, Lord,
　　but renew the Spirit in us, day by day,
　　　and in those who pray to you.

Penitence

Lord, full of compassion and mercy,
slow to anger and full of kindness and truth,
I have sinned, I have sinned, Lord, against you.
Alas, wretched person that I am, I have sinned against you!
Often and grievously have I sinned,
and have thought on things useless and vain,
and it was no good for me.

.. I hide nothing and offer no excuses.
    I give glory to you today.
I make confession against myself of all my sins,
    truly I have sinned against the Lord,
        and thus and thus have I done.
O alas, what things I have done, and you have not
    exacted the due reward of my sins,
        and it profited me nothing.

∴   And now what shall I say, or how shall I open my mouth?
        How can I answer to what I have done?
    Without excuse, without defence, I condemn myself.
        Yours, Lord, is the righteousness,
            and I am full of shame.
    You, Lord, are worthy in all
        that has come upon me,
for you have been true, and I have been sinful.

∴   And now, what is my hope. Is it not you, Lord?
        Yes, my hope is indeed in you
            if I have hope of salvation,
        if your loving kindness exceeds
            my disobedience.

O remember what my hope is.

Forsake not the work of your hands,
    your own image and likeness.
    Did you make it for nothing?
Yes, even for nothing if you forsake me:
and what profit is there in my going down to the pit?

Your enemies will rejoice over it.
O never let them rejoice over it.
    Grant not to your own enemies,
        to rejoice at my destruction.

Through the blood of your covenant
and in the release of the sins of the whole world,
    Lord, be merciful to me a sinner.
        Be merciful to me, O Lord,
    of sinners, the chief and the greatest.
            For the sake of your name
            be merciful to my sin for it is great,
                as great as it can be.

The Spirit is also helping our infirmities,
            and making intercession for us,
        with pleadings too deep for words:
    for the tender yearnings of the Father,
        the bleeding wounds of the Son,
    the unutterable pleading of the Spirit,

                Lord, hear,
                Lord, forgive,

Lord, listen and act, and do not hold back,
        for your own sake,
        Lord, Lord my God.

As for me,
I do not forget my offences,
they are ever before me,
    I reckon them up in the bitterness of my soul.
        I am anxious about them.
            I turn away and groan.
                I sense indignation,
                I feel revenge,
            I am weary of myself.
        I hate and blame myself,
that my repentance is not deeper, is not fuller.
    Yet, Lord, I repent, Lord, I do repent,
        help me in my unrepentance,

and more still, and more,
     pierce, rend, crush
          my heart.

Remit, pardon, and forgive me all things,
   whatsoever are to me a grief and offence of heart.
        O cleanse me from my secret faults!
Keep your servant from the sins I am unaware of.
      Show your wonderful mercies on me, the great sinner,
           and in due time say to me, Lord:
      Be of good cheer, your sins are forgiven you,
         my grace is sufficient for you.
              Say to my soul, I am your salvation.
Why are you so full of heaviness, O my soul,
             and why are you so disquieted within me?
        Turn to your rest, O my soul,
            for the Lord has rewarded you.

.   Lord, rebuke me not in your wrath,
            neither chasten me in your fierce anger.

..   I said, 'I will confess my
              transgressions to the Lord':
           and you forgave the guilt of my sin.

∴   O Lord, you know all my desires,
           and my sighing is not hidden from you.

∴   Have mercy on me, O God, in your great goodness:
           according to the abundance of your compassion
              blot out my offences.

∴∴   You will arise and have pity on me,
             it is time to have mercy upon me;
               surely the time has come.

.:.   If you, Lord, were to mark what is done amiss;
      O Lord, who could stand?

.:.   Enter not into judgement with your servant,
      for in your sight shall no one living be justified.

A prayer for grace

I lift up my hands to your commandments
      which I have loved.
    Open my eyes and I shall see,
incline my heart and I shall desire,
    order my steps and I shall walk
      in the way of your commandments.

    O Lord God, be my God,
and beside you let there be to me no other,
      no other person, no other thing, save for you.

Grant me
    to worship you and serve you
      in truth of spirit
      in graciousness of body
      in the blessing of speech
      both privately and publicly
    and to give

honour to those that have   { to obey   } them
   the rule over me   { to submit myself to }

and natural affection to my own { to care   } for them
                          { to provide }
to overcome evil with good
to keep my vessel in holiness and honour
to be free from the love of money

and to be content with the things that I have,
to follow the truth in love,
to desire not to lust
    not to lust to possess
    nor to pursue lusts.

The hedge of the Law

Help me:
        to bruise the serpent's head
        to consider my end
        to cut off the occasions
        to be sober
        not to sit down in idleness
        to shun the wicked
        to cleave to those who are good
        to make a covenant with my eyes
        to keep my body under control
        to give myself to prayer

Hedge round my way with thorns,
    that I find not the path
      for following vanity.
Restrain my mouth with bit and bridle,
for I am so unready to draw near to you.
O Lord, compel me to come in to be with you.

A Profession of Faith

I believe, O Lord in you

one God   {   Father
             Word
             Spirit

by your love and power
   all things were created

by your kindness and love towards humanity
   everything is gathered up
      in your Word
   who for us and for our salvation
      became flesh
      was conceived   born
      suffered   was crucified
      died   was buried
      descended   rose again
      ascended   is seated
      will return   will repay

   by the illumination and power
      of your Holy Spirit
     there has been called out of the whole world
       a special people,
to be a commonwealth in belief of the truth
       and in holiness of living:
     in which we are partakers
       of the communion of saints
        and forgiveness of sins
         in this world:
     that in it we are waiting
for the resurrection of the flesh
      and everlasting life
     in the world to come:

This most holy faith
which was once delivered to the saints
I believe, Lord:
O help my unbelief
and rescue the poverty of my faith.

Grant to me:
to love the Father for his tender love
to reverence the Almighty for his power
as a faithful Creator to commit my soul to him
in doing good;

from Jesus of salvation
from Christ of anointing
from the Son, only begotten of adoption

to worship the Lord

for his conception	in faith
his birth	in humility
his sufferings	by patience and all that
	has to do with sin
his cross	by crucifying the occasions of sin
his death	by mortifying the flesh
his burial	by burying under good works
	all my evil imaginings
his descent	by meditating on hell
his rising again	on newness of life
his ascension	by thinking of things above
his enthronement	to seek better things at his right hand
his coming again	in awe at his second appearance
judgement	by judging myself before I am judged

from the Spirit grant that I may receive the breath
    of his saving grace:
      in the church ⎫
         holy   ⎬ to share in ⎰ the calling
       catholic ⎭   ⎱ the hallowing
                                 the communion
   and a fellowship in the holy means of grace, by:
                      prayers   fastings
                      sighings   watchings
                      tears   sufferings
for the assurance of the forgiveness of sins,
    a hope of resurrection,
        and a crossing into eternal life.

Hope

The hope of all the ends of the earth
    and of those far away on the sea,
The one in whom our ancestors hoped
    and were their deliverer,
They put their trust in you and were not dismayed.

O you who have been my hope even from my youth,
      from my mother's breast,
         even from the womb:
           be my hope
              for ever and ever,
   and my hope in the land of the living.

for in your nature
   in your names
   in your types
   in your word
   in your dealings   is my hope

   let me not be disappointed
      in my hope.

Intercession

O you
    who are the hope of all the ends of the earth –
        remember for good the whole of your creation,
          visit the world with your tender mercies.
O you,
     who both died and rose again,
  so that you might be Lord of the dead and living –
       whether we live or die,
          you are our Lord,
        have mercy on us living and dead.

O helper of the helpless
    our timely help in trouble –
        remember all who are in need,
        and who need our help.

O God of grace and truth –
    strengthen all who are standing in truth and grace,
      restore all who are sick
        with heresies and sins.

O saving strength of your anointed –
    remember your congregation
      who you have purchased and redeemed long ago.
      O let the hearts of all believers
        again become one.

O Lord of the harvest –
    send out labourers, made worthy by you,
      into your harvest.

O you who are the portion of those who
      go into the sanctuary –
    grant to our clergy, rightly to divide the word of truth,

and to walk worthily in it.
Grant to the Christ-loving people
to be humble in attending to the truth.

O King of all nations to the end of the earth –
strengthen all the governments
of the world,
of your institution, but of the governance of man.
Scatter the nations that delight in war,
and make wars to cease
in all the world.

O Lord the hope of the islands, on whom the isles do wait –
deliver this island
and all the country where we dwell
from all tribulation, suffering,
and want.

Lord of Lords, Ruler of rulers –
remember all rulers
righteously appointed to rule over the earth.
And remember especially
our divinely appointed Monarch
and work mightily with him
and prosper his way in all things:
speak to his heart good things
on behalf of the Church
and of all your people.
Grant to him deep and undisturbed tranquillity
that we may live
in his peace
a quiet and peaceable life
with all godliness and honesty.

To the farmers and cattle feeders, good seasons,
to those in business not to overreach one another,

to mechanics lawfully to go about their work
and so down to the most humble of workers
and down to the poorest of the poor.

O **God** not of us alone, but also of our seed –
bless the children among us
that they may grow in wisdom as well as strength,
and in favour with you and with all people.

O you,
who will that we provide for our own
and hate those without natural affection –
remember those O Lord who are of our own flesh
grant me to speak peace concerning them,
and to seek to do them good.

O you,
who long for us to requite those
that do good to us –
remember Lord for good all those
who have been good to me,
keep them alive and bless all their days on earth.

O you,
who have written, that the one who is
careless of those who are his own, is worse than an infidel –
remember in your favour all my family,
peace to our home,
and the Son of peace be on all who live there.

O you,
who will that our righteousness
should exceed the righteousness of sinners –
grant to me Lord, to love again those that love me,
my own friends and my parents' friends,
and never to forget the children of my friends.

O you,
    who will us to overcome evil with good
      and to pray
  for those who hate us,
        have mercy on my enemies Lord, and on me
          and bring both them and me
            to your heavenly kingdom.

O you,
    who show favour to the prayers
      of your servants for each other,
        remember, O Lord, for good, and grant mercy
          to all those who remember me in their prayers,
          and all those whom I have promised to
            remember in my prayers,
          those who for good reason are unable to pray,
            remember them, O Lord, as if they did indeed
              pray to you.

O you,
    who count as accepted
      a ready mind in every good work –
        arise and have mercy on those who
          are in dire need, for it is time that
            you had mercy, indeed the time is come,
        and you will have mercy on them, Lord, as on me,
            even when I am in extremis.

the infants	hungry
boys and girls	naked
young people	sick
grown ups	prisoners
old people	strangers, friendless
all in extreme old age	unburied
and weakness	

those driven
>   towards self-destruction
>   troubled with evil spirits
>   sick in soul
>   and body
>   faint-hearted
>   the despairing

those in prison
>   and in chains
>   those condemned to death

>   orphans
>   widows
>   strangers

>   wayfarers
>   seafarers

> pregnant
> nursing mothers
> in bitter slavery in mines
>   galleys
> in remote places

You, Lord, shall save both man and beast.
>   How precious is your loving mercy, O God:
>   all mortal flesh shall take refuge
>   under the shadow of your wings.   Ps. 36.6, 7

Blessing

. The Lord bless us and keep us.
.. The Lord make his face to shine upon us
and be gracious to us.
∴ The Lord lift up his countenance upon us
and give us peace.

Commendation

I commend unto you, Lord,
my soul and my body,
my mind and my thoughts,
my petitions and all my prayers,
my senses and my members,
my life and my death,
my brothers, sisters, and all their children,
my friends and all who have done me good,
those commended to me,
my household and my neighbours,
my country and all of Christendom.

Praise and Thanksgiving

Beyond all being
Existence uncreate
Framer of the universe

God	Creator	Merciful
Jehovah	Possessor	Gracious
Most High	Deliverer	Slow to anger
Adonai	Redeemer	Plenteous in mercy
Almighty	Preserver	Keeping for thousands
Everlasting	Sanctuary	Forgiving iniquity and transgression

Living one who sees   Repenting of the evil
   Blessed   Praised
   Magnified   Extolled
Honoured   Hallowed   thy Holy Name

   for your Godhead
     infinity
     grandeur
     sovereignty
     Almightiness
     Eternity
     providence
God of truth   God of knowledge   God of forgiveness
   the Holy One   God of Hosts
Let Him be held in remembrance, lauded, extolled, honoured,
exalted.

   confidence
   place to flee to
   God

helper
who holds his shield over me
horn of salvation

Let us lift up our hearts to the Lord.
   It is indeed right and just,
fitting and our bounden duty,
in all things and through all things
at all times and in all places and ways   town and country
   always, everywhere, altogether,
     to remember you,
     to worship you,
     to proclaim you
     to praise you
     to bless, hymn, and to give you thanks
       for everything that is.

Creator, nourisher, preserver,
    guardian, governor, perfecter,
        Lord and Father,
        King and God,
            the fountain of everlasting life,
            the treasury of eternal goodness,
            whom the heavens praise with hymns,
                and the heavens of heavens,
           the angels and all the heavenly powers,
                do call continually
                one to another,
                and we too with them,
                lowly and unworthy
                beneath their feet,
            HOLY   HOLY   HOLY
                Lord God of hosts.
                Heaven and earth
                are full
            of the majesty of your glory.
        Blessed be the glory of the Lord
            rising from his place.

The Second Day:
Monday

In the morning you will hear my voice, Lord,
early I appeal to you, and look up.

Ps. 5.3

Commemoration

Blessed are you, Lord,
for you created:

the firmament of heaven,
the heavens, and the heavens of heavens,
the heavenly powers,
the angels, and the archangels,
the cherubim and seraphim.

the waters above the heavens,
mists, fog,
from whence
clouds from the ends of the earth
showers
dew
hail   lightning, thunder
snow as wool,   winds from the treasure store
hoar-frost as ashes storms
ice like morsels

the waters under the heavens,
for drinking,
and washing.

Confession

Of Moses

I will confess my sin   Lev. 26.40
and the sins of my ancestors,
because I have sinned against you, Lord,
forgotten and disobeyed you.
Set not my sins before you, Lord,   Ps. 90.8
my secret sins in the light of your presence,
but forgive the sin of your servant   Num. 14.19
as befits your great and constant love,
because you were merciful to me when I was young,
and have been even until now.

Of Job

If I have sinned, what harm can I do you, Job 7.20
you watcher of the human heart?
Why have you made me your target?
Why have I become a burden to you?
Why do you not pardon my offence,
and take away my guilt?
Reprieve me from going down to the pit, Job 33.28
for you have the price of release.   Job 33.24

Of the Canaanite Woman

Son of David have pity on me!   Matt. 15.22, 25, 27
Lord, help me!

True, Lord, and yet the dogs eat
 the scraps that fall
 from their master's table.

Of the Servant who owed ten thousand talents

Have patience with me, Lord.   Matt. 18.26, 25, 32
 Even more, Lord,
 I confess I cannot pay you.

Forgive me all my debt
I implore you.

A Prayer for Grace

Lord, guard me from
all impiety and profanity,
all superstition and hypocrisy,
worship of idols and worship of myself,
cursing and swearing,
neglect and irreverence in worship,
pride and carelessness,
argument and anger,
passion and corruption,
laziness and lying,
deceit and rudeness,
every wicked thought,
every unclean imagination,
every base desire,
every inappropriate imagining.
and, Lord, grant me:
godliness and holiness,
the spirit of worship and adoration,
kind speech and the keeping of my vow,
attentiveness in the holy place,
loyalty and adaptability,
patience and kindliness,
chastity and temperance,
contentment and gentleness,
truthfulness and integrity,
a pure imagination.

A Profession of Faith

I believe in God
1   = Father – almighty – creator $\left\{ \begin{array}{l} \text{heaven and} \\ \text{earth} \end{array} \right.$

2   and in   .   Jesus
             .. Christ
             ∴ only begotten Son
             ∵ our Lord

    1   conceived by the Holy Spirit
    2   born of Mary ever virgin
    3   suffered under Pontius Pilate
    4   crucified
    5   will come again from there
    6   to judge the living and the dead

3   and in the Holy Spirit
       the Church
    1   holy
    2   catholic
    3   communion of saints
    1   forgiveness of sins
    2   resurrection of the flesh
    3   life everlasting

Hope

And now what is my hope? Is it not in you, Lord?   Ps. 39.8
      Truly my hope is in you,
        for in you, Lord, have I put my trust.   Ps. 31.1
      Let me never be put to shame.

Intercession

Let us ask of the Lord

for   the whole creation ⎰ healthful
        the chorus of seasons ⎱ fruitful
                               peaceful

for   all people everywhere
        ⎰ non-Christian
        ⎱ Christian
for   those departed, refreshment and light
        for the living, conversion
        for those in trouble, restoration
                from their sickness and sin,
            and confirmation of those
                    given truth and grace
                        by you;

for   the help   ⎧ dejection
        and consolation of ⎨ sickness
        men and women in   ⎪ hopelessness
                            ⎩ restlessness

        for thankfulness
        and moderation   ⎧ cheerfulness
        of men and women in ⎨ health
                            ⎪ resourcefulness
                            ⎩ peace of mind

for   the Church catholic
                its stability and increase
        Eastern
                its safety from violence and its growth
        Western
                its perfection and pacifying

British
>   restoration of things wanting in it
>   strengthening of things that remain

for   the Episcopate – the Presbyterate – the Christloving laity

for   the Government   .   of the world
>   ..   Christian and far away
>   ∴   near at hand
>   ⸪   among ourselves

for   those in authority
>   our own divinely guarded Monarch
>   those eminent in the Palace
>>   Council, Judges, Army, and Forces.
>>   Leaders of the people
>   husbandmen, farmers, fishermen,

>   merchants, traders, workers
>   and so on down to the lowest crafts
>>   beggars

for   the Succession
>   for the good education of the Royal Family
>>   of the children of the nobility
>>   those in   Universities
>>   Inns of Court
>>   Schools
>>   at work in   cities
>>   in fields

for   **those commended to me by**
>   kindred,
>   brothers, sisters
>   for the blessing of God on them and their children

benefits received
   requite all those by whom
      I have ever been benefited
         or who have helped me in the things of this world

those whom I have had in my charge
      those I have taught
         those ordained by me
      my college   my parish
    the Church of Southwell
         of St Paul
         of Westminster
   Dioceses of Chichester
          Ely
   my present Diocese
clergy, laity, officials, governors,
the Deanery of the Chapel Royal
   the office of Almoner
   the Colleges entrusted to me

my friends
   those who love me
      some unknown to me

Christian love
   as for those who hate me without a cause
      and for others who do so even for truth
         and righteousness' sake

the neighbourhood
   for those who live quietly and harmlessly
         next to me

my own promise
   as for those whom I have promised

to remember in my prayers

mutual concern
> and for those who remember me in their prayers
> and who ask the same from me

want of leisure
> and for those unable to pray for good reason

for   those who have none to intercede for them
> for these in particular

for   those who at this time are struggling
> in extreme situations of necessity

for   those who are leading any reform
> through which glory may come to your Name
> or some greater good to the Church

for   those who are doing good works for religion
> or for the needy

for   those for whom I have been a stumbling-block.

Blessing and Commendation

God be merciful to me
> and bless me:
cause your face to shine upon me
> and be merciful to me.
> God, even our own God,
>> bless me, O God.

Accept my pleading,
> direct my life in the way of your commandments,

        sanctify my soul,
             purify my body,
                  correct my thoughts,
             and cleanse my desires.

In my soul and body,
        mind and spirit,
             heart and feelings,
        renew me through and through, Lord,
             for if you will, you can.

Praise

Lord, Lord ,', ,',   Exod. 34.6, 7
  2   God
  3   merciful
             and
  4   gracious
  5   slow to anger
             and
  6   ever faithful
             and
  7   true
  8   remaining faithful
         for thousands
  9   forgiving iniquity
 10   and rebellion
 11   and sin
 12   but without acquitting
             the guilty
 13   visiting the iniquity
         of the fathers on the children

        I will bless the Lord at all times   Ps. 34.1
      his praise shall ever be in my mouth.
             Glory to God in the highest,   Luke 2.14

and on earth peace,
goodwill to all people.

Lord, we praise you for:

in their

Angels ⎫		abiding
Archangels ⎬ Col. 1.16		illumination
Virtues ⎪		miracles
Thrones ⎭		judgement
Sovereignties		generosity
Principalities		government
Powers		over demons
Cherubim		wisdom
Seraphim		love

Lord, we praise you

In every
    imagination of our heart
    word of our lips
    work of our hands
    and every path that our feet take.

The Third Day:
Tuesday

O God, my God, early will I seek you.

Ps. 63.1

Commemoration

Blessed are you, Lord,
who by drawing the water into sea,
caused dry land to appear
and let the earth produce growth of plants
and fruit-bearing trees.

From the **Abyss** came
    the depths ⎫
            ⎬ as in a bottle
    the sea ⎭
lakes, rivers, springs.

From that which was **without form** came
    earth, continents, islands,
    mountains, hills, valleys,
    farmland, meadowland, woods.

From the **Void** came
    green things,
        corn for bread,
     grass,
           herbs and flowers:
          for food,
             pleasure,
                healing,

trees
>   yielding fruit
>> fruits   wine
>>>   oil

>>>>   spices
>>   for wood;

things under the earth   stones
>>   metals
>>   and minerals
>>>   coal,
blood and fire and a turmoil of smoke

>>>>>   Joel 2.30

Confession

. Of David

> Who can tell how often they offend?
>> Cleanse me from my secret faults.
>> Keep your servant from sins committed unawares,
>> and, for your name's sake,
>> let them not get dominion over me.
>>> Forgive my sin,
>>>> for it is great.

> My sins have overtaken me
>> and I cannot see.
> They are more in number than the hairs of my head,
>> and my heart fails me.
> Be pleased, Lord, to deliver me.
>> Lord, make haste to help me.
> Show me your marvellous loving-kindness,
>> O Saviour of those who take refuge at your right hand.
> I said, Lord be merciful to me,
>> heal me, for I have sinned against you.

.. **Of Solomon**

    I have sinned

       and I am ashamed,

          but I turn from my sinful ways,

          turn to my heart,

          and with all my heart, I return to you,

             seeking your face,

               and praying to you, saying,

   I have sinned, I have done wrong, I am wicked.

      I know, O Lord, the plague of my heart,

      and look, I turn to you

         with all my heart and with all my strength.

    Now, O Lord, from where you dwell,

      and from the throne of the glory

        of your kingdom in heaven,

          hear the prayers

            and the pleadings of your servants.

    Forgive your servant,

      and heal his soul.

∴ **Of the Publican**

    O God, have mercy on me, a sinner.

      Be merciful to me,

         the chief of sinners.

∴ **Of the Prodigal**

    I have sinned against heaven and against you.

      I am no longer worthy to be called your son.

        Treat me as one of your hired servants,

          make me one of them, even the lowest,

         the least among them all.

A Prayer for Grace

to forgive me

for   fantasy

error

trespass

sin

transgression

iniquity

abomination

O Lord, work in me

seriousness

clearing myself of blame

indignation

longing

devotion

eagerness to see justice done

2 Cor. 7.11

A Profession of Faith

I believe in the

Godhead of the Father

friendship

power

providence

Salvation of the Son

anointing

Sonship

Lordship

conception

birth

sufferings

cross
death
burial
descent
resurrection
ascension
enthroned
return
judgement

Breath of the Holy Spirit

holiness
 the calling out of the ⎫
 the hallowing in of the ⎬ Universal
        ⎭
communion of saints
and of saintly things
forgiveness of sins
resurrection
life eternal

Hope

O Lord, be to me a hope,
for you are the hope of all the ends of the earth,
and of the farthest seas.

Ps. 65.5

Intercession

Creatures
> People
> those who have died before us
> those who are still alive
> those who are overcome by illness

Churches
> the Catholic Church the Episcopate
> the Eastern the Presbytery
> the Western the Clergy
> the Church of these lands the Christ-loving Laity

Nations
> of the world
> Christian
> neighbouring
> our own

Leaders
> Monarchs
> Godly Princes
> our own

Councillors
> Judges
> Magistrates
>
> Commanders on { land
> sea

The People
> the Succession those commended to me
> the teaching body formerly or now
> those in the Palace **by:**
> cities friendship

country
those concerned with souls
bodies
nourishment
shelter
health
the necessities of life
birth
kind actions

love
neighbourhood
my own promise
mutual discussion
those without leisure
extreme need
the last agony

Blessing

Watch over me, Lord,
and be my defence on my right hand.
Guard me from all evil.
Keep my soul, O Lord.
Watch over my going out
and my coming in,
from this time forward,
and for evermore.

Ps. 121.5, 7

Commendation

Lord, you know, you are able, and you will
the good of my soul,
(wretched person that I am).
I do not know, nor am I able, (nor
as I ought) do I will that good.

But you, Lord, I pray to you,
in your boundless loving-kindness,
so to direct and guide me,
in the way best pleasing to yourself,
and most suitable for me.

Praise

Goodness   2 Thess. 1.11
   grace
      love

   kindness   Titus 3.4

love of people

meekness   2 Cor. 10.1
   gentleness

forbearance   Rom. 2.4
   long suffering

mercy   . much
        .. and great
compassion
       . multitude of compassion
       .. tender hearted compassion
     tender kindness
     abundant tenderness

in passing over
   overlooking
      many times
      many years

   unwillingly
     not willingly
   not fully
   not according to   Ps. 103.10
   not forever   Ps. 103.9
   in wrath, mercy
   repenting of the evil   Joel 2.13

double   Isa. 40.2
to pardon
    reconcile
    readmit

The Fourth Day:
Wednesday

In the night watches I think of you, O Lord,
for you have been my helper.

Ps. 63.7, 8

Commemoration

Blessed are you Lord

who created two sources of light $\left\{\begin{array}{l}\text{sun}\\\text{moon}\end{array}\right.$

       great and less
     and the stars
  for . light
     .. signs
     ∴ seasons   spring summer autumn winter
∴ and to rule over day   days
        and night   weeks
                 months
                 years

Confession

of   Isaiah

Behold, you showed your anger, for we have sinned.
We have all become like something unclean,
    and all our righteousness
      is like a filthy rag.

We wither as leaves, and all our iniquities
    carry us away like the wind.

Now, Lord, you are our father,
    and we are the clay,
        and all of us are the work of your hands.

of   Jeremiah

You, O Lord, are among us
    and we bear your name,
        do not forsake us.

of   St Paul

Lord I am of the flesh
    sold as a slave to sin.
What dwells in me (in my flesh that is)
    is in no way good.

I want to do good
    but I do evil.

I consent to the law that is good
    and I delight in it in my inmost self,
    but I see another law at work in what I do,
    a different law,
    warring against the law of my mind,
    and making me a prisoner under the law of sin.

O wretched creature that I am!
Who will release me from this body of death?

I thank God through Jesus Christ,
    that where sin did multiply,
    there grace did abound.

O Lord your grace leads me to repent,
    and gives me a change of heart,
    releasing me from the clutches of the devil
      in which I am trapped.

of   St Peter

Let my past life suffice me,
    doing the will of my own desires,
living in licence, debauchery, drunkenness,
    orgies and carousal.

Lamb, without spot or blemish,
you have redeemed me
by your precious blood:
    and in that very Name,
    beside which there is none under heaven
    given to us,
    by which we must be saved.

A Prayer for Grace

from the	pride	**of the**	Amorite
	envy		Hittite
	anger		Perizzite
	gluttony		Gergazite
	lust		Hivite
	worldliness		Canaanite
	lukewarmness		Jebusite

Grant me
    humility of mind
    pity
    patience
    temperance

chastity
contentment
eagerness of zeal

A Profession of Faith

I believe
in the Father   kindly affection
       the Almighty   saving power
       the creator   providence
for the saving, guiding, perfecting of the universe.

in Jesus   salvation
       Christ   chrism
       the Only-Begotten   adoption
       Lord   service

his conception ⎱
his birth   ⎰ for the cleansing of our unclean ⎰ conception
                                                                ⎱ birth

his sufferings, that he bore, so that we did not:
       cross   the curse of the law   ⎱
       death   the sting of death   ⎰ all taken away
       burial   hopeless corruption in the tomb ⎰

his going down where we should, that we might not:
       his rising up as the first fruits of those who slept:
       his ascending to prepare a place for us:
       his enthronement to appear and intercede for us:
       his judgement to render to each according to their works.

in the Holy Spirit   power from on high
            outwardly and visibly   transforming us
            powerfully and clearly   into holiness

in the Church   the mystical body
  of those called out of the world
  into a citizenship of faith and holiness.

in the communion of saints   the members of this body
  a mutual sharing in holy things
  for the assurance of the forgiveness of sins
  and for the hope of resurrection
     of translation

Hope

As for me, my trust is in your mercy
 from age to age.
How excellent is your mercy O God.
 If I have hope it is in your mercy.
Let me not be disappointed of this hope.

Intercession

We pray to you O Lord:
Remember all for good,
 have mercy on all, O sovereign Lord,
  be reconciled to us all.
  Pacify the multitudes of your people
  scatter offences
  bring wars to an end
  stop the uprising of heresies
  grant to us your peace and love,
  O God our saviour,
  you who are the hope of all the ends of the earth.

Remember to crown the year with your gladness
 for the eyes of all wait on you O Lord,
  and you give them their food in due season:
   you open wide your hands
   and fill all things living with plenty.

Remember your holy Church
 that is from one end of the earth to the other,
 and bring her peace,
  which you have bought by your own blood,
 and established, even to the end of the world.

Remember those who bear fruit and do good work in
 your holy churches, and are concerned for the poor and
   those in need.
  Recompense them
   with your rich and heavenly gifts.
    Give them

for things	earthly	things heavenly
	corruptible	incorruptible
	temporal	eternal

Remember those who are in virginity, and poverty,
        and discipline,
 and those who live in holy marriage
  in piety and in awe of you.

Remember every Christian soul
 afflicted and oppressed and struggling,
  and needing your mercy and help;
 and our brothers and sisters who are held in captivity
  or in prison, in bonds, or in degrading slavery.

End the schisms of the churches,
 quench the furious ragings of the people,
  and receive us all into your kingdom,

making us children of light,
and bestow your peace and love on us.

O Lord our God

Remember, O Lord, all spirits and all flesh
whom we have remembered,
and whom we have not remembered,
from righteous Abel, down to this day.
As for us, direct the end of our lives
to be Christian and well-pleasing,
(and if it be your will) painless and in peace,
gathering us together at the feet of your elect,
when you will and how you will,
only without shame or sin.

Blessing

The glorious majesty of the Lord
be upon us:
and prosper the work of our hands
upon us,
and prosper our handiwork.

Be Lord

within	**me**	to sustain	**me**
without		preserve	
over		shelter	
beneath		support	
before		direct	
behind		bring back	
round about		strengthen	

Blessed are you Lord God of Israel,
our Father.

Yours Lord is the greatness
   the power
   the glory
   the victory
   and the praise
for all that is in heaven and earth is yours.
  Every nation and every kingdom
   trembles at your presence.
  Yours Lord is the kingdom
and you are exalted above all
  and above every nation.
  From you is their wealth
and their glory from your face.
  You, Lord, reign over all
  the ruler of all who rule,
and in your hand is power and might,
and in your hand is to make great
  and to give strength to all.
Now therefore, Lord, we exalt you
  and praise your glorious name.

The Fifth Day:
Thursday

Satisfy us early with your mercy, Lord.

Ps. 90.14

Commemoration

Blessed are you
  who brought forth from the waters
    moving creatures with living souls,
      whales,
    and birds that fly,
    and you blessed them
  so they should increase and multiply.

THE ASCENSION
Be exalted above the heavens, O God.

By
  your resurrection
    draw us to yourself, Lord,
  that we may set our hearts
    on things above, not on things on the earth.

By
  the spiritual mystery of your holy
    body and precious blood
      in the evening of this day.

By
  the birthday of your
    humble servant,
    Lord have mercy.

Confession

. of Ezekiel

As I live (said the lord God)
I have no pleasure in the death of a sinner,
but that the wicked should turn from their wickedness and live.
Turn, turn from your wicked way,
for why will you die, O house of Israel?
Turn us to yourself, Lord,
and so we shall be turned.
Turn us from all our sins,
and let them not be our ruin.

.. of Daniel

I have sinned, I have done wrong,
I have done wickedly,
against your precepts and your judgements.

Yours Lord is the righteousness,
and mine is the confusion of face,
as today, because of the rejection,
with which you have rejected us.

Lord, to us belongs the confusion of face,
and to our princes because we have sinned against you.
Lord, in all things is your righteousness,
let your anger and fury be turned away,
and let your face shine on your servant.

O Lord, turn your ear, and listen.
Open your eyes and look on my sorrow.
Lord, hear. Lord, forgive. Lord, listen.
Listen, Lord, and act. Do not delay,
for your own sake, loving God,
because your servant has called your name.

∴ **of James**

    In many things we go wrong again and again.

    Lord, let your mercy rejoice against your judgement
        concerning my sins.

∴ **of John**

    If I say I have no sin I deceive myself
        and the truth is not in me,

    but if I confess my sins $\begin{cases} \text{many} \\ \text{grievous} \end{cases}$

    You, Lord, when I confess

are faithful and just to forgive me my sins.

    Even for this I have an Advocate with you,
        and to you,

your own Son, the Only-Begotten, the Righteous.

    May he be the propitiation,

who is the propitiation for the whole world.

A Prayer for Grace

to turn us from:

    every weight
        and besetting sin,
    all obscenities
        and excess of evil,
    desires of the flesh
            eyes
    pride of life,
        every motion, both of flesh and spirit,
            which goes against
                your holiness.

so that I may be:

.   poor   in spirit   so that I may inherit the
                                  Kingdom of Heaven

..   sorrowful   so that I may be comforted

∴   meek   that I may inherit the earth

∴   hunger and thirst ⎫
·   aft. righteousness ⎭   that I may be filled

⁖   merciful   to obtain mercy

⁚   pure in   ⎫
⁚   heart   ⎭   that I may see God

⁙   a peacemaker   that I may be called a child of
                                  God

      persecuted   ⎫
⁙   for the cause of ⎬   so that my reward may be
         right   ⎭   in heaven

A Profession of Faith

Coming to God
I believe that he is,
and that he rewards those who seek him
                    diligently.

I know that my redeemer liveth
    that he is the Christ, the Son of the Living God,
    that he is truly the Saviour of the world,
    that he came into the world to save sinners
        of whom I am the chief.

Through the faith of Jesus Christ we believe we shall be saved,
    in the same way that we believe our ancestors were.

I know that my flesh shall be raised up
    that has endured these things.

I believe that I shall see the goodness of the Lord,
    in the land of the living.
In the Lord shall our heart rejoice,
    for in his holy name we have put our hope
        the Name
            of the Father,
                Saviour   :   Mediator   :   Intercessor
                            Redeemer

        of the twofold Comforter ⎰ the Lamb
                                 ⎱ the Dove
        Let your mercy, O Lord, be upon us,
            as we put our trust in you.

Intercession

In peace let us pray to the Lord
for the peace that is from above and for the salvation
                                        of our souls.

for   the peace of the whole world
    and for the good estate of the holy churches of God
        and for the union of them all;

for   this holy house and for those who with faith
    and reverence enter in;

for   our forebears in holy things, for the worthy
                                        presbyterate,
        for the deacons ministering in Christ,
                            and for all the clergy
            and people;

for   this holy house and all the city
              and country, and for all believers who live here;

for   the good temperature of the air, abundance of the fruits
              of the earth, and peaceful times;

for   those at sea, those travelling, the sick,
              the weary, the prisoners and for their deliverance.

              Help, save, pity, and protect us,
                  O God, by your grace
              all-holy, undefiled, highly blessed
              Mother of God, and ever-virgin Mary
              together with all the saints, we commend
              ourselves, each other and all our life
                  to Christ our God, even to
                      YOU LORD
              to whom be glory, honour, and worship.

              The grace of our Lord Jesus Christ
                  and the love of God
              and the fellowship of the Holy Spirit
                  be with me, and with us all.
                      Amen.

      I commend myself, and all mine, and all that I have
              to him who is able to keep us from falling,
      and to present me faultless before the presence of his glory:
          to the only wise God and Saviour
              to whom be glory and majesty
                  dominion and power
                      both now
                      and unto all
                          ages.

Thanksgivings

O Lord, my Lord

for   that I am
         that I am alive
         that I am rational

for   my   upbringing
                safety
                guidance

for   my   education
                civil rights
                religion

for   your   gifts to me $\begin{cases} \text{of grace} \\ \text{nature} \\ \text{world} \end{cases}$

for   my   redemption
                rebirth
                teaching

for   my   calling
                recalling
                repeated recalling back to you

for   your   forbearance
                long-suffering
                continued long-suffering towards me
                       many times
                       many years

for   all the benefits
                    which I have received
              for any to whom I have done good

for the use of the present blessings of this life,
for your promise
for my own hope,
and for the enjoyment of things
to come.

for   my parents honest and good
gentle teachers
benefactors always to be remembered
like-minded, religious friends
listeners of intelligent mind
sincere friends
faithful servants

for   all who inspire me
by their writings
their sermons
conversations
prayers
examples
reproofs
or misdeeds

for   all these and also for all other mercies
which I know of and of which I do not know
open and secret
remembered by me, and forgotten,
kindness received by me, willingly
or against my will.

I praise you, bless you, and thank you
and I will praise, bless and thank you
all the days of my life.
Who am I, and what is my father's house,
that you should look on such a dead dog as me?
What reward shall I give unto the Lord:

for all his benefits to me?
What thanks can I give back to you, O God,
for all the things which
you have spared me
until now?
and carried for me.

Praise

Holy   Holy   Holy
Worthy are you, O Lord our God, the holy one,
to receive glory and honour
and power,
for you have created all things,
and by your will they are,
and were, created.

The Sixth Day:
Friday

Early in the morning my prayer shall come before you.

Ps. 88.13

Commemoration

Blessed are you, Lord
   who created from the earth, wild animals and cattle,
      and all reptiles $\left\{\begin{array}{l}\text{food}\\\text{clothing}\\\text{help}\end{array}\right.$ for
  and you made human beings
    in your image
    to rule over the earth
    and blessed them

  the fore-counsel
    fashioning hand
  breath of life
    image of God
    the setting over works
    charge to the angels concerning them
    Paradise

heart	life	knowledge of God
loins	sense	writings of the law
eyes	reason	sayings of the prophets
ears	spirit	melody of the psalms
tongue	free-will	instruction of the proverbs
hands	memory	lessons from the histories
feet	conscience	offering of worship

Blessed are you, Lord,
    for your great and precious promise
    on this day, concerning the life-giving good,
       and when the time was ripe on this day,
          for the fruition of the same.

Blessed are you, Lord, for your holy sufferings
       on this day.
By your saving sufferings on this day
       save us, Lord.

Confession

of   **Hosea**

I have stood out against you, O Lord, but I return to you.
I have fallen by my unworthiness
but I bring with me words
and return to you, saying,
    forgive my sin and receive my prayer,
    and I will give you the fruit of my lips.

of   **Joel**

Spare, Lord, spare,
and do not expose your own people to insult
    among your enemies.

of   **Amos**

Lord, Lord, be gracious; hold back, I beseech you.
    Who shall raise up Jacob
       for he is small?
    Repent over this, O Lord,
      let this not be.

of   **Jonah**

Clinging to false gods and lies

I rejected mercy
and was thrust away from your eyes.
But when my soul fainted within me,
I remembered the Lord,
and still will I look toward your holy Temple,
for you have saved my life from the pit.

of   Micah

Who is a God like you who pardons the sins
of the remnant of your people?
You will not always let your anger rage,
for to be merciful is your true delight.

Turn again and have mercy on us, Lord,
wash away our guilt,
and cast all our sins into the depths of the sea,
in your truth and in your mercy.

of   Habbakuk

I have heard of the report of you
and am afraid.
I have considered your works
and stand in awe.
In your anger, remember mercy.

of   Zechariah

Look upon me, Lord, see my filthy garments.
See Satan standing at my right hand,
and, O Lord, in the blood of your covenant
in the fountain opened for the sprinkling
of all impurity,
take away my sin from me,
and wash away the sin that clings to me.
Save me, like a burning coal snatched from the fire.

Father, forgive me; for I did not know,
truly I did not know what I was doing
when I sinned against you.

Remember me, Lord, in your kingdom.

Lord, do not hold this sin against my enemies.

Lord, lay not my sins to my charge.

By the sweating of great drops of blood,
the agony of your soul,
your head crowned with thorns
driven in with the blows of the stick,
your weeping eyes,
your ears filled with reproaches,
your mouth receiving drink of vinegar
and gall,
your face defiled with shameful spitting,
your neck loaded with the
burden of the cross,
your back ploughed with stripes and
wounds from the scourge,
your hands and feet nailed through,
the loud cry, *My God, My God,*
your heart pierced with a spear,
the water and the blood that flowed,

body broken
blood outpoured

Lord, forgive the sins of your servant,
cover all his sins,
remove all your displeasure,
turn from the fierceness of your anger.

Turn me, O God of our salvation,
  and turn away your anger from us.

Will you be angry with us for ever?
  Will you stretch out your anger from one generation
                                    to another?
O God, will you not turn again and give us life,
  that your people may rejoice in you?

Show us your mercy, Lord,
  and grant us your salvation.

Ps. 85.1–6

A Prayer for Grace

to guard me against:
The sins of the flesh

adultery	hatred	sedition
fornication	discord	heresies
uncleanness	jealousies	envy
lust	anger	murders
idolatry	strife	
witchcraft		

drunkenness, disorder, and such like.

and, O Lord, grant me:
The fruits of the Spirit

love	longsuffering	faithfulness
joy	kindness	humility
peace	goodness	temperance
wisdom	counsel	knowledge
understanding	might	fear of the Lord

The gifts of the Spirit
  the word of wisdom
    word of knowledge

    faith $\begin{cases} \text{gifts of healing} \\ \text{working of miracles} \end{cases}$

    prophecy
    discerning of spirits
    varieties of tongues
    the interpretation of tongues

A Profession of Faith

I believe
. that you created me:
    despise not
      the work of your hands.

.. that I am made after your image and likeness:
    let not your own likeness be defaced.

∴ that you saved me by your blood:
    let not the price of the ransom
      be squandered.

∴ that you proclaimed me Christian in your name:
    let not your namesake be scorned.

.∴. that you hallowed me in rebirth:
    let not that consecration be despoiled.

:: that you engrafted me into
    the cultivated olive tree:
      let not the limb of your mystical body
        be cut out.

Hope

Remember your word to your servant,
  on which you have built my hope.
My soul is pining for your salvation;
  I have hoped in your word.

Intercession

Let us pray:
  for the right guidance and strengthening
    of all Christian people,
  for our ancestors in holy things,
    and for all our companionship in Christ,
  for those who hate us, and those who love us,
  for those who show kindness and minister to us.
  for those who we have promised to remember
          in our prayers,
  for the deliverance of captives,
  for our absent brothers and sisters,
  for those who are sailing on the sea,
  for those who are stricken with sickness,

Let us pray
      for the abundance of the fruits of the earth
  and for every soul of all worthily believing Christians.

  Let us bless devout monarchs and leaders,
        the orthodox pontiffs,
        the founders of this holy place,
          our parents,
  and all those who have gone before us.

Praise

Be unto me always, Lord,
    your strong hand for defence:
your mercy in Christ
    for salvation:
your all-true word
    for instruction:
and the grace of your life-giving Spirit
    for comfort,
       to the end
         and in the end.

soul of	Christ	sanctify	
body		strengthen	
blood		release	
water		wash	me
stripes		heal	
sweat		refresh	
wounds		hide	

The peace of God
    which passes all understanding,
keep my heart and mind
in the knowledge and love of God.

O Lord, when they broke your commandment and fell,
    you did not despise nor reject them,
but as a tender Father, you visited them
       in so many ways,
granting them your great and precious promise
    with the life-giving seed,
    opening to them the door of faith,
      and of repentance into life.

In the fullness of time
      you sent your Christ
   to take on the seed of Abraham,
   and in the offering of his life
   he fulfilled, in perfect obedience
   and in the sacrifice of death,
   a ransom for the whole world,
and in his rising again, he gave us life.

   O Creator of all things,
your will is to return us to yourself,
      that all should be partakers
of your divine nature and eternal glory.

O you who have witnessed to the truth of your gospel,
   in many and diverse showings of your power,
   in the ever memorable conversation of your saints,
   in their supernatural patience in suffering,

      blessed, praised, celebrated,
      magnified, exalted, glorified,
      hallowed be your name, the recalling,
   the memory, and every memorial of it,
            now and for ever.

   .   Worthy are you to take the Book
         and to open the seals,
   for you were slain and redeemed us for God
         by your blood
   from every tribe, tongue, people and nation.

   ..   Worthy is the Lamb that was slain
         to receive power and riches and wisdom,
         strength, honour, and glory, and blessing.

∴   To him who sits on the throne and to the Lamb
         be blessing and honour, glory and power
            unto ages of ages. Amen.

∴   Salvation to our God who is seated on the throne
         and to the Lamb.

∴   Amen,
         blessing and glory and wisdom,
  and thanksgiving and honour and power,
      and strength, be to our God,
         for ever and ever.

The Seventh Day: Saturday

Lord, be gracious to us, because we have trusted in you.
Be our arm every morning,
and our salvation in the time of suffering.

Commemoration

Blessed are you Lord,
for you rested on the seventh day
from all your works,
and you blessed them and hallowed them.

Concerning the Sabbath:
our recurring rest,
the burial of Christ,
the ceasing from sins,
and those who have gone before us
into their rest.

Confession

Of Ezra
O my God, I am ashamed
to lift up my face to you.
My sins tower over me
and my guilt is so great
it reaches to the heavens.

From the days of my youth until now,
I have been in great error,

and because of this,
    I cannot stand before you.

Of Manasseh

I have sinned
    more in number than the sand of the sea:
    and I am not worthy to look at the height of heaven
        for the number of my sins,
        nor have any release,
        for I have provoked your anger
        and done evil in front of you
        nor have I kept your commandments.

So now I bow the knee of my heart,
    to beg for grace from you.
I have sinned, Lord, I have sinned,
    and I acknowledge my faults.
        Yet I ask you most humbly,
            forgive me Lord, forgive me,
        and do not destroy me through my sins.
        Do not be angry for ever,
            by reserving evil for me,
nor condemn me to the lower parts of the earth.
        For you are the God, even the God of those who repent,
            and in me you will reveal all your goodness.
            For, unworthy as I am, you will save me
                according to your great mercy,
                    and I will praise you for ever.

Sir, if only you will, you can make me clean.	Matt. 8.2
Lord, you need only say the word, and my servant will be cured.	Matt. 8.8
Teacher, we are sinking! Do you not care?	Mark 4.3
Say to me, take heart my child; your sins are forgiven.	Matt. 9.2
Jesus, Master, have mercy on me.	Luke 17.13

Son of David, Jesus, have pity on me
   Jesus, Son of David
      Son of David.   Mark 10.47, 48
Lord, say to me, 'Ephphatha', 'Be opened'.   Mark 7.34
Sir, I have no one.   5. John 7
Lord, say to me, you are rid from your trouble.   Luke 13.21
Say to my soul, I am your salvation.   Ps. 35.3
Say to me, my grace is all you need   2 Cor. 12.9

A Prayer for Grace

    to guard me against
         all the

failures	debts
shortcomings	sins
slips	neglects
falls	
trespasses	ignorance
stumblings	impieties
	uncleanness

the guilt
condone, pardon, forgive
remit
spare
be merciful to
lay not to the charge of
impute not
remember not

the disgrace
pass by
pass over
look away from, overlook
cover
wash away
blot out
cleanse

the hurt
put up with
heal
save from

take away
take off
strip off
bring to nothing
set aside
disperse
let them not be found
let them not exist

O Lord, supply

to my faith	virtue
virtue	knowledge
knowledge	temperance
temperance	patience
patience	godliness
godliness	charity
charity	love

that I forget not that I was forgiven my former sins,
but may have diligence to make my calling, and my election,
        sure, through good works.

A Profession of Faith

I believe in you, the Father.
    See then, if you are a Father, then we are
            your children,
        and as a father loves his children, so have pity on us.

I believe in you, the Lord.
　　See then, if you are Lord and we the servants,
　　　　our eyes look to you, O Lord
　　　　　　until you have mercy on us.

I believe that if we were neither children nor servants,
　　but dogs only,
　　　　still it would be lawful for us to eat the crumbs
　　　　　　that fall from your table.

I believe that Christ is the Lamb of God,
　　O Lamb of God, who takes away the sins of the world,
　　　　take away mine.

I believe that Jesus Christ came into the world to
　　　　save sinners.
　　You who came to save sinners, save even me
　　　　the chief and greatest of sinners.

I believe that Christ came to save those who were lost.
　　O you who came to save those who were lost,
　　　　never allow those to be lost, whom you have
　　　　　　saved.

I believe that the Spirit is Lord and Giver of life.
　　You who gave me a living soul,
　　　　grant that I may not have received my soul in vain.

I believe that the Spirit gives grace in sacred things,
　　pray that I may not have forfeited the grace of them,
　　　　nor the hope and promise of a blessing through them.

I believe that the Spirit prays for us
　　with a yearning that cannot be spoken.
In those prayers, and in that yearning,
　　allow me to share.

Hope

In You our ancestors have hoped,
>they hoped and you have delivered them.
They cried out to you and were saved,
>in you they put their hope, and were not cast down,
>as with those in former times,
>so deliver us, O Lord.

Intercession

O Heavenly King
strengthen our faithful monarchs
>establish the faith
>calm the nations
>give peace to the world
>protect this holy place
set the members of our family
who have gone to their rest before us
>in the tabernacles of the just,
and we who come to you in good faith
>and with true repentance, receive you,
O good and gracious lover of your people.

Blessing

Strength of the Father   shepherd me
Wisdom of the Son   enlighten me
Power of the Spirit   quicken me

Commendation

Guard my soul
   strengthen my body
   make tender my senses
   direct my behaviour
   tune my character
   bless my actions
     complete my prayers
     inspire my thoughts
the sins committed previously   forgive
       the present correct
       the future prevent

Thanksgiving

To Him who has strength to do all things
   far above all we can ask or think
  through the power that works in us,
     to Him
  be glory in the Church in Christ
    to all generations
    unto ages of ages.
    Amen.

blessed   praised   extolled
magnified   exalted   glorified

hallowed
be your name, O Lord and remembered
  and the memory and every memorial of it

for the
  patriarchs   all-honourable senate
  prophets   ever-venerable choir

apostles   all-illustrious company of twelve
evangelists
martyrs   noble army
confessors   assembly
teachers
ascetics
virgins   beauty
children   the sweetening of the world

for their
        faith
        hope
        labours
        truth
        blood
        zeal
        seriousness
        tears
        purity
        godliness

Glory to you, O Lord, glory to you,
    glory to you who glorified them
in whom and for whom we also glorify you.

Great and marvellous are your works
    O Lord God, Almighty,
    Just and true are your ways,
        O King of the nations.

Who will not fear you, O Lord,
    and glorify your name
  for you alone are holy
    and all nations shall come
  and worship before you,
for your righteous acts stand revealed.

Praise our God all you his servants,
  and you that fear him both small and great,
      Alleluia!

  For the Lord is become King,
      even our God the Almighty.
  Let us be glad and rejoice
      and give honour to him.

Behold! God pitches his tent with mankind,
      and he will dwell with them.
          They shall be his people
      and God himself shall be with them.
          He shall wipe away all tears
              from their eyes.
          There shall be no more death
                  nor crying
      neither shall there be any more pain
          for the former things
              are passed away.

Prayers
at the End of the Day

An Evening Reflection

The heart is deceitful above all things.
The heart is deep and full of windings.
The old man is covered up in a thousand wrappings;
therefore keep guard over yourselves.

Make these matters your business

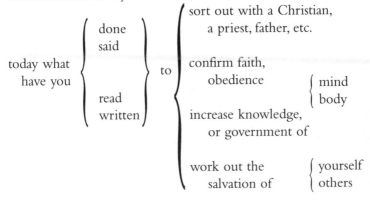

today what
have you
{ done
said
read
written }
to
{ sort out with a Christian,
a priest, father, etc.

confirm faith,
obedience { mind
body

increase knowledge,
or government of

work out the { yourself
salvation of { others }

We see even God himself closing the several days
of the first creation with a review of the works of each day,
And God saw that they were good.

Gen.1.31

Commemoration

Departed and gone is the day,
I give you thanks, O Lord.
Evening beckons me,
make it bright.

There is an evening,
as of the day so also of life.
The evening of life is age,
age has overtaken me,
make it bright.

Turn me not away in time of age;
do not forsake me when my strength fails me.
Even to my old age be the one,
be the one who makes me, bears me,
to carry and deliver me.

Abide with me, Lord,
for it is toward evening
and the day is far spent
of this busy life.
Let your strength be made perfect
in my weakness.

The day is fled and gone,
going also is life,
the life, lifeless.
Comes the night
and so does death,
the death, deathless.
As the end of the day draws near,
so too the end of life.
Remember us we pray,
so the end of our life

may be Christian, acceptable,
faultless, blameless,
and, if it please you, painless.

In peace lay us down,
Lord, Lord,
gathering us together
at the feet of your chosen ones,
when you will and as you will,
only without shame and sin.
Let us remember the days of darkness
for they shall be many,
lest we be cast into outer darkness.

Let us remember to overcome the night
by doing some good thing.
Judgement is close:
a good and acceptable answer
at the awesome throne
of JESUS CHRIST,
grant us, Lord.

Thanksgiving

By night I lift up my hands in the sanctuary
and bless the Lord.
The Lord has granted his loving kindness
in the day-time,
and so through the night his song will be with me.
I will make my prayer to the God of my life.
I will bless you as long as I live,
and lift up my hands in your name.
Let my prayer rise before you as incense,
the lifting up of my hands as an evening sacrifice.
Blessed are you, O Lord our God,

the God of our ancestors,
who created the changes of days and nights,
has given us songs in the night,
and delivered us from the evil of this day,
nor have you cut short my life,
like a weaver her cloth,
nor from day through to night,
made an end of me.

Confession

LORD,
as day upon day,
so sin upon sin;
seven times a day the just man falls,
but I, an exceeding great sinner,
seventy times seven.
It is a dreadful thing, O Lord,
but I turn with groaning
from my evil ways,
and I return into my heart,
and with all my heart I turn to you.
God of those who turn, and Saviour of sinners,
evening after evening I will return
in the innermost marrow of my soul.
From the depths my soul cries out to you:
I have sinned, Lord,
grievously sinned against you
oh, the misery,
I repent, oh I repent, spare me, Lord,
I repent, oh I repent,
help me in my failure to repent.

Be gentle, spare me, Lord.
Be sparing and forgive me.
I said, Lord be merciful to me,
heal my soul for I have sinned against you.
Have mercy on me, O God, in your great goodness,
according to the abundance of your compassion
blot out my offences.

Remit the guilt,
heal the wound,
blot out the stains,
clear away the shame,
rescue from the tyranny,
and do not make me a public example.

Bring me out of trouble,
cleanse me from my secret faults,
keep your servant also from presumptuous sins.
The wanderings of my mind,
my idle speaking,
lay not to my charge.
Remove the dark and muddy flood
of foul and wicked thoughts.
O Lord,
my destruction comes to me of myself,
whatever things I have done amiss, mercifully forgive,
deal not with us according to our sins,
nor reward us according to our wickedness.
Look mercifully on our infirmities;
and for the glory of your all-holy name
turn us from all the evils and troubles
which by our sins, and by us through them,
are most rightly and worthily deserved.

Commendation

In my tiredness, Lord,
give me rest.
In my exhaustion, renew my strength.

Lighten my eyes, that I sleep not in death.
Deliver me from the terror of this night,
and the danger that stalks in darkness.

Grant me a healthy sleep,
that I may pass through this night without fear.

O Keeper of Israel,
who neither slumbers nor sleeps,
guard me this night from all evil.
Guard my soul, O Lord.

Visit me with the visitation of your own,
reveal to me Wisdom in the visions of the night,
and if not, for I am not worthy, not worthy,
at least O loving Lord,
let sleep be to me a breathing time,
from toil, and from sin.

Nor let me in my dreams, dream
what may anger you,
or spoil me.
Let not
my passions be filled with fantasies.
Let my conscience strengthen me through the night,
and free me from grievous terror.
Preserve me from the black sleep of sin.
Put to sleep
all evil and earthly thoughts
within me.

Grant me to sleep lightly
rid of all fantasies
fleshly and satanical.
Lord, you know
how sleepless are my unseen enemies,
and how feeble my wretched flesh,
for it was you that made me.

Shelter me under the wings of your pity.
Wake me at the fitting time,
the time of prayer,
and help me seek you early,
for your glory and your service.

Into your hands, O Lord, I commend myself,
my spirit, soul, and body.
You made them, and redeemed them,
together with me, my friends,
and all things mine.
You have given them to me, Lord,
in your goodness.

Preserve my lying down and my rising up,
from henceforth, now, and for ever.
Let me remember you upon my bed
and search my spirit.

Let me wake and be with you,
let me lie down in peace, and take my rest,
for it is you, Lord, only
that make me dwell in safety.

The Lambeth Palace
Manuscript

A Meditation on the Passion

PRAISE, BLESSING, AND THANKSGIVING

for the death of Christ,
in his obedience unto the death of the cross:
for the things which he suffered,
in his being pressed on every side:

in ⎰ Gethsemane
   ⎱ Gabbatha
     Golgotha

      the pains, pangs ⎱
      the shame   ⎬ of the cross
      the curse   ⎰

that he willed   1   to be betrayed by his own disciple
                   2   sold for 30 pieces of silver
                      1   vexed in soul
                      2   very weary
                      3   full of anguish
                      4   exceedingly sorrowful, to death
                      5   in agony
                      6   to utter a loud cry
                           shed tears
                      7   sweat blood like dew on the earth

that   1   his disciples should fall asleep
                          to be betrayed by a kiss
                  2   that his disciples should flee
                          to be left alone
                  3   denied by a strong oath
                          and by a curse

4 subjected to the powers of darkness
   1 seized by hands
   2 arrested as a robber
   3 tied up
   4 dragged off to
      1 Annas
      2 Caiaphas
      3 Pilate
      4 Herod
      5 Pilate again
      6 the Praetorium
      7 Gabbatha
      8 Handed over
      9 Golgotha
     10 Cross

1 Annas and Caiaphas
2 Accusation
3 False witness
4 Condemned of blasphemy
   1 derided in many ways, insulted by servants
   2 beaten up
   3 slaps of the hand
   4 blindfolded
   5 beaten
   6 spat at
   7 jeered at
   8 blasphemed

Pilate
1 accused of sedition
2 to be denied at the end
3 to be replaced by Barabbas
4 to be hounded to the cross by the will of the crowd

Herod
1 dressed him in a gorgeous robe
2 treated him with contempt
   sent him back to Pilate

1   renewed demands for his death
2   to a very shameful death
3   handed over to the will of the soldiers
4   dressed in scarlet
5   a stick for a sceptre
6   a crown of thorns
7   falling on their knees they jeered
8   they called him king in derision
9   they spat at his face
10   beat him about the head

1   to a pillar
2   beaten with sticks
    scourged
    a baptism of blood
    bruises
    wounds
    Behold the Man!   (a grievous sight)
    Away!   *Crucify!*
    His blood be on us
    sentence of death

to be loaded with the cross
   to sink
   to be given myrrh to drink
   stripped   shame
               grief
   stretched on the cross
   fixed with nails
   hands and feet pierced
   set in between thieves
   and one of them repenting

   to be mocked by the passers-by
   to be blasphemed by one of the thieves

My God, my God
to be derided when he called on God
to thirst
to be given vinegar to drink
to bow his head
to give up his spirit
to have his side pierced with a spear
when dead to be called a deceiver

Father forgive
Mother, behold your son
Today, with me
My God, my God
I thirst
It is finished
Father, into your hands

1 the precious death
2 the opening of the side
3 blood and water
4 the begging of the body
5 the taking down from the cross
6 the burial in another's grave
7 for three days
   1   triumph over cosmic powers
   2   mighty resurrection
  Appearance to Magdalene
  to the women
  to Peter
  to those going towards Emmaus
  to the ten without Thomas
  to the eleven with Thomas
  at the Sea of Tiberias
  to James
  to the five hundred
  (Transfiguration)

3   the glorious Ascension
4   seated at the right hand
5   distribution of gifts
6   standing up on our behalf   as an advocate
                                 as priest
7   the turning to bless for the second time
8   the judging of the living and the dead

Prayers based on
The Lord's Prayer

1   **The Name of the Lord**
is holy and held in reverence
    by all: and by some
much more than others, and by me principally
    more than many.
But I have not so held it, nor to those close to me
    am I what I am known to be.
Woe to me wretched soul that I have not,
    I frankly confess. I ache from the soul.
Humbly I ask for pardon,
    humbly for grace,
that from now on I will speak, act, and live
    that your name may be hallowed
· by others, because of me.

2   **Your Kingdom** is the head
of all my prayers,
    and that I may come to it in a state of glory
    let it come to me here, in a state of grace.
    So that in the kingdom there
    I may find a place, even the least,
    at the feet of your saints.

3   Let the will of the flesh $\left.\right\}$ go from me
    of human stock

and your will $\left\{\begin{array}{l}\text{holy}\\\text{righteous}\\\text{gracious}\end{array}\right\}$ be done $\left\{\begin{array}{l}\text{by this earth}\\\text{from this earth}\end{array}\right.$

in me
as it is in heaven.

4   **Give** what things are for   health
                                         peace
                                         sufficiency
       Give the bread of angels for eternal sufficiency.

5   **Forgive me my debts**
           the huge sum of debts
           shameful falls
           frequent relapses
           daily wallowings
       To you, O Lord, belongs justice,
           and to me confusion of face.
       My destruction is my own fault.
       If you, Lord, will be extreme to mark what is done amiss,
       Lord who may abide it?
       But there is mercy with you,
       with God there is mercy,
       and with God there is plentiful redemption,
       and he will deliver us from all our sins.

       Free me, O Lord, from mine,
       free my soul from the deepest hell.
       Deep calls to deep, and delivers from the deep.
       But there are other things as well which I feel less,
           but are no less serious.
       I ask you to let me know these,
           so that I can confess them.

6   **And lead me not**
           Do not let me be led.
           into temptation
           mindful of, and pitying, my fragility
           and weakness, so many times proved.

7   **But deliver me from evil**
    evil in myself and the flesh
        and the surprises of it,
    evil of the devil and its promptings,
    evils of punishment which I have justly
        and worthily deserved,
    evils of the world to come
        these spare, here burn, here cut, Lord,
    evils of the present world
        here also spare,
    evils of this world and things
        that happen in it,
    evils of this disease with which I struggle,
    evils of business with which I am entangled,
    evils of past, present, and future:
    from all these deliver me, O Lord,
        and save me, your servant for ever,
        even the least among the least.

    I beseech you, O Lord, in your mercy,
turn from me your righteous indignation
        while so often and so badly,
        so badly and so often,
        I have sinned against you,
    especially recently, lately,
        I have sinned against you.
Turn your indignation from me, from parents, sisters,
    my Reverend Father in the Lord, and family;
        those I know, friends, neighbours,
        country, Christian people the world over.
        Amen.

Occasional Prayers

Penitence for everything, always

In whatever way from my childhood onward,
right up until now,
known of, or ignorant of,
within or without,
sleeping or waking,
in words, deeds, or thoughts,
through the subtle darts of the enemy
through the sinful desires of my worldly nature,
that I have sinned against you:
have mercy on me and forgive me.

In Praise of the Nature and Work of the Holy Trinity

God, Father of heaven,
who wonderfully created the world out of nothing,
and by your goodness sustains and guides heaven and earth,
you handed over to death for us your Only-Begotten:

God the Son, Saviour of the world,
you desired to be born of a Virgin,
your precious blood washed away our sins,
you rose from the dead, victoriously
and ascended into heaven:

God the Holy Spirit, Comforter,

you came down on Jesus in the form of a dove
and you came in tongues of flame on the Apostles,
and by your grace you come down and confirm
the hearts of the saints:

holy, highest, eternal Trinity,
beautiful, blessed,
good Father,
loving Son,
kindly Spirit,
whose work is life, whose love is grace,
and whose contemplation is glory,
I adore you with all the affection of my heart,
and I bless you now and for ever.

A Prayer for the Living and Departed

O God,
your majesty is ineffable,
your power incomparable,
your goodness inestimable.
You are the Lord of the living and the dead.
We are those whose power in the world
is bound in the flesh.
They are those, whose bodies are laid aside
and are now received.
Give to the living, mercy and grace,
and to the departed, rest and light for ever.
Give to the Church, truth and peace,
and to us, forgiveness of sins, and your good favour.

A Thanksgiving for the Gifts of God

We thank you, gracious Lord, for
opening the eyes of the blind,
setting the prisoners free,
clothing the naked,
lifting the fallen,
healing the broken-hearted,
gathering the dispersed,
giving food to the hungry,
raising the dead to life,
casting down the mighty,
lifting up the lowly,
proclaiming liberty to the captives,
giving us timely help in distress.

To Live and Die Well

O Lord,
calm the waters of my fear,
and kindle the flame of my love,
that I may know you keenly,
and follow you faithfully,
to live well and to teach well,
Living and dying always in your grace,
grant that in all your commandments
I may never be separated from you.
And so allow me that good end
which is above every gift,
and if it be your will,
set me a place beside you,
so that with the saints I may praise you.

A Good and Holy Life

Grant Lord,
a glorious and joyful resurrection:

who gave to Ezekiel fifteen extra years of life
give me so much space of life
at least to the extent
that during it I may deplore my sins:
who sped the way of Abraham by the leading of an angel
and the Magi's journey by the leading of a star,
who preserved Peter on the stormy waters,
and Paul in the shipwreck:
be with me Lord
and speed me on my way:
lead me out, lead me along, lead me back.
Give me soundness of mind,
wholeness of body
grant mildness of air,
yield fruits of the earth,
restore the sick to health,
bring back the lapsed,
to those travelling on sea or land
a good journey and a safe harbour;
joy in suffering, a lifting up of the oppressed,
the freeing of prisoners:
allow.

Addressing God

Let my prayer ascend
come to you
enter in
be placed in your sight

find grace
come before you
that it may not return to me empty
but in the way that you know, and are able, and are willing
hear
turn your ear
reach out
consider
understand
discern
hear, in order to act,

O Lord, do not
turn away, hide your eye, avert your gaze, turn your face,
cover yourself with a cloud
hold back your peace
sleep, be far from me, reject me,
cast me away from your presence,
despise, desert, leave me at the end,
take your love away
mislead with vanities
let your anger pass all bounds
forget me at the end, sweep me away with sinners,
betray me
rebuke me in your anger, punish me with your wrath.

A Prayer of the Passion

You who before your judge was silent,
guard my mouth;
You who willed to be tied with ropes,
guard my hands;
You who willed your glorious body to be wounded,
by it forgive those sins
which I have committed with my head;

You who willed your holy hands to be pierced,
by them forgive whatever sins I have committed
by unlawful touch, or by unlawful operation;
You who willed your precious side to be pierced,
by it forgive whatever I have done by unlawful thoughts
in the heat of passion;
You who willed your beautiful feet to be tied
by them forgive what I have done wrong
by the paths my feet have trod, swift to do evil;
You who willed your whole body should be stretched out
by your body forgive whatever sin I have done
in my whole body.

And I, Lord, am wounded in soul.
Look! the great number,
the length, the breadth, the depth
of these wounds
from head to foot.
So by yours, heal mine.

For God's delight in all I do

O put into my mouth, speech
that is true and well-pleasing,
that I may give delight
in all my words
in my bearing
and in all I do,
for those who see and hear:
that I may discover grace,
in all my public speech and prayer.

A Conclusion to Prayer

Together with those for whom I have prayed,
or for whom I am in any way bound to pray,
and with all the people of God,
it be granted to me
to be brought into your kingdom,
to appear there in righteousness,
and to be filled with glory.

Fragments

would that
would rejoice if
I am afraid
sorry that not

whether
good or bad
I am yours always

For Grace and Mercy

Let not the fault of the flesh,
but let your mercy profit me.
Let not your anger come upon me,
but let your grace I pray go before me.
Show me mercy
now, and in the hour of my death.

In Christ

Let me so receive these mysteries
that I may be worthy
to be grafted into your body, the church,
that I may become one of your members
and you my head;
that I may remain with you and you with me,
not I in myself
but you in me and I in you,
and you my Head,
and so forever continue
in the unbreakable bond of love.

For the Gift of Tears

My dryness, O my dryness,
I am dried up, like a piece of broken pottery.
O Lord, increase what I have,
supply what I have not
of the fountain of tears.

So often failing, what face, what mind
shall I now be able to show?
None: so utterly confused am I, in my confusion.
I walk, I sit, I throw myself down,
beating that heart of mine
that does not beat me enough.

Lord, give. It is in you to give.
You can turn rock into running water.
Give me tears. Make my head a fountain.
Give me the grace of tears.
Drop down you heavens from above,
and moisten the dryness of my desert.

Give, Lord, this grace.
No other gift
not great riches
nor any of the good things of the world
can equal the grace of tears,
like David's, or Jeremiah's
or Mary Magdalen's, or Peter's
(his in bitterness).

Make my eyes to weep
leave them not like hard flint,
but if you will, one drop at least,
and then another as well,
for your bottle,
for the book.

But what if I cannot manage even that?
O pumice!
Oh! lime, boiling
in freezing water...
At least of Christ's tears
grant me some.

A Confession based on
The Ten Commandments

Lambeth Palace MS 3708, pp. 38–57

O deliver not thine own inheri=
tance into the will of the enemy.

Ld carest thou not that I perish?
    I am thine, O save me.

Behold o Ld how that I am thy servant
    I am thy servant the Sonne of thy
    hand mayd, thy unprofitable ungrateful
    ~~hand mayd~~ Servant, yet thy Servant
    thy unkind lost child, yet thy child
    Though I have not returned the dutiful
    kindnesse of a sonne, yet doe thou not thou
    cast from thee the kindnesse and compassion
    of a father.

Ld I have not denyed thy name, but
    confessed it aloud & in the confession of
    it, and invocation thereof I desire
    to spend my last breath.

o Ld I have prepared my heart to
    meet thee, though not accordinge
    to the rule of thy Sanctuary.

o Ld I believe, helpe my unbelief.

o Ld I freely forgive, whomsoever
   I have anything against.

o Ld I have patiently born whatsoever
   thy hand layeth upon me for me
   for my chastisement.

o Ld I come unto thee weary and heavy
   laden, thou hast bid me come, thou
   hast promised him that cometh to thee
   that thou wilt nott cast him out.

I have sinned but I hide it not
   excuse it not, like it not.

I will confesse my wickednesse & be
   sorry for my sin. My confusion
   is dayly before me, & the
   shame of my face hath covered me.

I am the Lord thy God: Thou shalt have
none other gods but me.

1 I have touchinge thee o Ld been full
   of rovinge imaginations & evill
      thoughts.

  I have not studied to seek & know
  thee as I ought, knowinge
    that I have not glorified thee nor
  been thankful to thee accordingly.

  I have doubted of thy promise and not
  trusted to thy helpe.

  I have made flesh mine arme and

hoped for prosperitye rather from
    man than from thee.

Thou shalt not make to thyself and graven image . . .
Thou shalt not bow down to them or worship them

2 I have neglected invocation and a=
    doration or not performed it
    with the duty and reverence that I should.

I have not been thankful especi=
    ally not for thy chastisements.

I have not worshipped thee in
    Spirit and in truth.

I have been more carefull of the
    outward ceremonial part of
    thy worship than of the inward
    and spirituall.

I have desired much to thee on my
    lips, but my heart hath been
    farre from thee.

Thou shalt not take the Name of
the Lord thy God in vain: for the Lord will not
hold him guiltless, that taketh his Name in vain.

3 I have not spoken of thy name
    with due regard.

I have not given occasion to others
    to sanctifye thy name, but ra=
    ther by my evill life, it hath
    been evil spoken of.

I have not duly reverenced and re=
    garded those things whereon
        thy name is imprinted.

I have with rash oaths and eager ex=
    ecrations oft abused thy holy
        name.

Remember that thou keep holy
the Sabbath day. Six days shalt thou labour,
and do all that thou hast to do; but the seventh
is the sabbath of the Lord thy God.

4   I have not brought to thy pub=
    lick service the care and reverence
        that becomes me.

I have not spent the dayes conse=
    crate thereto in holy exercises.

I have upon no sufficient cause
    absented myself from thy holy
        assemblies.

I have upon those days intended
    my own private business.

I have been content in them with the
    use of the means alone, with out
        any practise at all.

Honour thy father and thy mother;
that thy days may be long in the land which the
Lord thy God giveth thee.

5 I have not so reverently spoken
nor so dutifully carried my
selfe, towards some as thou hast
placed over me, as was meet I
should.

I have not so carefully prayed
for them as was requisite.

I have not opposed to those who have
unreverently spoken of them,
Chiefly of those who had in go=
vernment touching my soule.

Thou shalt do no murder.

6 I have not wished and provided
the good of my neighbour as I
should, but rather maligned   beene
angry and quarrelled with them
and sought revenge upon every light
wronge.

I have not had that compassion on the
poor that I should nor ministered to
their necessities.

I have not defended them against the
wrong of others as I might.

I have not rejoiced in the good suc=
cess of my neighbour, but envyed
his well fare.

Thou shalt not commit adultery.

7   I have not possessed my vessell
        in holiness and honour, nor preserv=
        ed it from pollution as the Tem=
        ple of the Holy Ghost should be.

   I have not eschewed the occasions of
        lust, nor made that covenant with
            mine eyes as I should.

   I have suffered my fancy to wander
        too licentiously.

   I have not brought under my bodye
        nor kept it in subjection with
            such abstinence as I should.

   I have more studiously intended
        with more cost my flesh than my
            Spirit.

   I have not so kept mine ears and
        tongue as I should.

   Thou shalt not steal.

8   I have not been content with mine
            owne estate, but wished an
                higher.

   I have not been so exact in pay=
        inge and dealing with those I
        have dealt with all as in justice
        I was bound.

   I have with undue means interver=
        ted to mine owne use that which
            was not mine.

I have not of that I had more than
enough been willinge to part
with to the relief of the needye.

Thou shalt not bear false witness
against thy neighbour.

9 I have not been so studious of
speakinge the truth as I should.

I have desired to seeme & to be
respected more than I was.

I have not had the care of the good
name of my brother, as I was
bound.

I have not so hated flattery as
I should.

I have not so stood and defended the
the truth as was meet I should.

Thou shalt not covet thy neigh=
bour's house, thou shalt not covet thy neigh=
bour's wife, nor his servant, nor his maid, nor
his ox, nor his ass, nor any thing that is his.

10 I have been full of wandering de=
sires, wicked affections, unlawful
concupiscenses, evil suspicions &
surmises, immoderate lusts touching
my neighbour, and that which is his.

O remember not the sinnes and
offences of my youth.   Ps. 3.7
For youth & childhood are
but vanities.   Eccl. 17.10

To live
        without   necessity
        above   contempt
        below   envye